PALMERSTON

PALMERSTON

DENIS JUDD

INTRODUCTION BY
A.J.P. TAYLOR

WEIDENFELD AND NICOLSON
LONDON

To Kate

© Denis Judd 1975

Designed by Behram Kapadia
for George Weidenfeld and Nicolson Ltd
11 St John's Hill, London SW11

ISBN 0 297 76706 2

Printed in Great Britain by
Butler & Tanner Ltd, Frome and London

CONTENTS

LIST OF ILLUSTRATIONS

between pages 88 and 89

INTRODUCTION

PALMERSTON is a special case among British prime ministers, a
sort of nineteenth-century Churchill. Over seventy when he
attained the supreme office, he was carried to power by his
individual reputation, not by the workings of the party system.
He began as a Tory, became a Whig, and ended as the first
Liberal prime minister without ever changing his political
outlook or beliefs. He was called to power during the Crimean
war as the saviour of his country and duly carried it to victory,
as Chatham had done before him and Lloyd George and
Churchill were to do after him.

He was in the full sense a 'character', remembered with
admiration a generation after his death. His jaunty, casual air
was misleading, though it struck the popular imagination. He
was in fact extremely hard-working, holding one office or
another for forty-eight out of his fifty-eight years in Parliament.
As Foreign Secretary, he wrote all his dispatches in his own
hand and instituted an orderly system of records for the first
time. His foreign policy was all his own. He did not listen to the
permanent officials and rarely troubled to consult the Cabinet.
He combined, as perhaps no other Foreign Secretary has done,
maintenance of the balance of power and support for
constitutional states in Europe. Metternich hated him; there
could be no higher testimonial.

Others before him had won fame by their oratory in the
House of Commons. Palmerston, a somewhat slapdash speaker,
took a leaf out of the Radicals' book and played deliberately for

the support of public opinion. He was the first politician of eminence to 'work' the newspapers. He cultivated editors and still more proprietors, whom he duly rewarded with honours. He wrote leading articles himself day after day even when in office, often reproducing his official dispatches word for word. His colleagues were baffled and exasperated by his popularity. They could not understand that Palmerston had turned from the great families to the man on the top of the Clapham omnibus.

Palmerston had another resource as prime minister, one less regarded and yet destined to become a powerful weapon in the political battle. It was in his time, it seems, that honours were regularly distributed in exchange for contributions to the party funds. The old aristocrats had relied on family influence. The new capitalists put their hands in their pockets, and Palmerston abetted them, despite being something of an aristocrat himself. In all his acts he was impudent – cheeky in his speeches, daring in policy, Lord Cupid when he was young, Lord Pumicestone when he was old. He was not an original thinker or a creative statesman. He was in politics for fun, and no prime minister has provided it more abundantly.

A. J. P. TAYLOR

I

THE ROAD TO WESTMINSTER
1784-1809

HENRY JOHN TEMPLE, third Viscount Palmerston, was born at 7 p.m. on 20 October 1784. Great Britain had just emerged from the trauma of the loss of the thirteen American colonies; Dr Johnson was translating Horace, Sir Joshua Reynolds dominated the Royal Academy and Edward Gibbon was well into the fifth volume of his *Decline and Fall of the Roman Empire.* In the same year the Prince of Wales, the future Prince Regent, was mooning over the forbidden Catholic fruit of Mrs Fitzherbert, and the twenty-five-year-old William Pitt the Younger, prime minister for less than a year, had inspired some robust lines:

> Chatham, thank heaven! has left us a son;
> When *he* takes the helm, we are sure not undone;
> The glory his father revived of the land,
> And Britannia has taken Bill Pitt by the hand.

The infant Henry John Temple was the eldest child of the second Viscount Palmerston. The Temples were an old-established English family who had first risen to prominence in the reign of James I. During the Civil Wars, Sir John Temple had been an ardent Parliamentarian and an outspoken supporter of Cromwell's bloody Irish campaign in 1649; as a result of these

1

loyalties he was awarded lands confiscated from dispossessed Irish Catholic landowners. Sir John had successfully trimmed his convictions under Charles II, and his son in turn emerged from the 1688 Glorious Revolution and its aftermath with his Irish estates much enlarged. In 1723 Henry Temple, Sir John's grandson, was given an Irish peerage and became the first Viscount Palmerston.

The Temples were now guaranteed a secure position in the aristocratic firmament of eighteenth-century England, and, if they wished, an appropriate involvement in political activity. The first Viscount lived at his father's house in East Sheen, and also bought Broadlands in Hampshire as a second country seat. He derived a comfortable income from rents of land in Ireland and England, and drew a sinecure clerkship in the Court of the Exchequer worth £2000 a year. As an Irish peer he was able to sit as an MP in the House of Commons.

In 1757 he was succeeded by his grandson, the second Viscount, who lived until 1802. The second Lord Palmerston was elected to the House of Commons at the age of twenty-two and remained an MP for the rest of his life. His political interests were not particularly profound, and, though a close friend of the radically-inclined Charles James Fox, he was a steadfast supporter of the Treasury benches rather than of the Opposition, a tradition nobly maintained by his illustrious son, the third Viscount, who contrived to hold office for forty-eight of his fifty-eight years in the House of Commons.

The second Viscount begot his son and heir comparatively late in life. Although he had married at the age of twenty-seven, within two years his first wife died a few days after the birth of a still-born baby. After fourteen years as a widower he married, when he was forty-three years old, Mary Mee, the daughter of a London merchant living in Dublin. The circumstances of their meeting were unorthodox and more than appropriate in view of the amorous proclivities subsequently displayed by their first-born. The second Viscount had fallen from his horse in Dublin and had been carried for sustenance to the nearby house of Benjamin Mee. There the daughter of the house, Mary, had nursed her aristocratic patient back to health and had received a proposal of marriage into the bargain. In January 1783 she became Lady Palmerston.

The marriage proved both happy and fruitful. Lady Palmerston bore her husband five children in rapid succession: Harry in October 1784, Fanny in February 1786, William in January 1788, Mary in January 1789 and Elizabeth in March 1790. Of these, all lived into adulthood save Mary who died as the result of a smallpox inoculation in 1791.

Although Harry, the future prime minister, lived a remarkably active and demanding life until his death two days before his eightieth birthday, as a child he was considered to be delicate. Fourteen months after his birth, however, he was described as 'a fine, eager, lively, good-humoured boy'.

Shortly before his fifth birthday the future master of foreign affairs was taken on a six-week tour of Belgium and the adjoining German states. The whole family left England in September 1789, scarcely two months after the fall of the Bastille had set up reverberations that were to run the length and breadth of Europe. The Palmerstons' trip, however, had a cultural, rather than a political character. Lord Palmerston was keenly interested in science and the arts, a friend of Garrick and Sheridan, a patron of the theatre, a dabbler in astronomy, and a fairly indifferent versifier, as his lines *On Beauty* show:

> A cheek that shames the vernal rose,
> A breast that vies with mountain snows;
> A mouth that smiles with matchless grace,
> Like pearls within a ruby case.

He was also an intrepid collector of paintings and sculpture, and the family tour that ended on 2 November 1789 was largely devoted to this passion.

Two years later, in 1791, the second Viscount undertook a mission to Paris, on behalf of Charles James Fox, to meet the moderate leaders of the Revolution. He noted with unease the breaking up of the great estates of the French aristocracy, and generally deplored the trend towards revolutionary egalitarianism. But he still managed to cast an eye over some French paintings, as well as over Emma, the newly-acquired wife of the ambassador-designate to Naples, Sir William Hamilton, en route for Italy.

Undeterred by the progress of the Revolution, Lord Palmerston decided in 1792 to take his family on a two-year holiday to Europe while his new London house in Hanover Square was being enlarged. The Palmerstons reached Paris on 1 August. Danton had called for revolutionary forces to come to Paris and the Palmerstons were greeted by a large detachment just arrived from Marseilles and bawling a marching song that was soon to become world-famous. Despite this ominous mustering of southern Jacobins, King Louis XVI and Marie Antoinette still shakily held court at the Tuileries, and Lord and Lady Palmerston were presented to them there.

Lady Palmerston, however, had become convinced that the family should leave Paris as soon as possible and return 'when liberty is not at such a height'. On 7 August they set off in two coaches: the first coach, containing Lord and Lady Palmerston and Harry, passed through the barricades of the revolutionary Faubourg St Antoine district, but the second coach carrying the younger children and the servants was halted by the mob, and was only allowed to proceed after being questioned. Three days later, on 10 August, the Tuileries fell to the revolutionary militia and the fate of the royal family was sealed. In September the French Republic was proclaimed.

As the Palmerstons rode south towards Switzerland they

gradually shook off the uncomfortable manifestations of the Revolution. There is no reason to suppose that the young Harry Temple acquired any deep distaste for Jacobinism from his first-hand contact with its power, though his father's convictions on the subject were doubtless reinforced by the family's experiences in Paris. During the next two years of his continental travels, Harry was subjected to other, more pacific influences: he saw the court of the Two Sicilies at Naples, where Lady Hamilton was now ensconced as a favourite of the Queen; as well as mastering French, he learnt to read and write Italian fluently, through a tutor, Signor Gaetano; he stayed in some of the great cities of Europe – Lausanne, Turin, Bologna, Rome, Naples, Berne, Venice, Innsbruck, Munich and the Hague.

There were less happy occurrences, too. In Verona, in September 1793, he fell victim to a serious attack of fever which held up the family's progress for three weeks. Events in France were, moreover, pushing Europe towards the two decades of war that were only terminated upon the field of Waterloo in 1815: in January 1793 Louis xvi was executed, and Britain promptly went to war with revolutionary France. On 2 October, while a British army under the Duke of York was campaigning in the Netherlands, the Palmerstons arrived home again. Seven months later Harry was sent to Harrow.

Harrow school in May 1794 was almost exclusively a preserve of children from the moneyed classes, quite contrary to the intentions of its Elizabethan founder John Lyon. The curriculum was top-heavy with classical Greek and Latin, though gambling, fist-fighting, heavy drinking, bullying and ferocious discipline were more universal hallmarks of life at Harrow than academic excellence.

Lord and Lady Palmerston probably chose Harrow for their son because his grandfather Benjamin Mee had been there, and had even won a prize for archery. Lady Palmerston, however, concerned for the delicate health of her first-born, fretted over the type of bed he was to occupy and insisted that he wore nightshirts. Her fears, though understandable, proved groundless. Harry bathed in the nearby river, hunted rabbits, played cricket, took part in an easily-overawed school mutiny, and became celebrated in a school song for his 'frame of iron'. He also acquired a high reputation for fisticuffs, and on one occasion a flustered Mrs Bromley (his housemaster's wife) tended his black eye and bleeding nose after he had fought 'a great boy called Salisbury, twice his size'. There was also the frequently repeated tale of his pillow-fight victory over George Gordon, the future Lord Aberdeen, whom Palmerston was to replace as prime minister during the Crimean War.

The young Harry Temple's letters to his parents and his friends show that from the first he found Harrow to be agreeable enough. Shortly after his arrival he dutifully told his mother and father that 'I like the Scool very much . . . I am well and hope to continue so, for I am in a very healthy place'. Doubtless his mother's anxieties were soothed by this tactful reference to his salubrious surroundings. He also showed an appropriate interest in food from home, writing lovingly of a cake that was very 'much liked – what I liked best in it was that at top it was plain and at bottom plumb, and then the sugar was so rich'. Animals were also important to him: he mourned the loss of a ferret, and later wrote that 'a man came here today with a nest of hedgehogs. If I had known where to put it, I should certainly have bought one to keep Fanny's [his sister's] guinea-pig company, for he must be very solitary'.

Unlike the solitary guinea-pig, Harry's life at Harrow was remarkably full. He advanced steadily through the Removes of the Fourth Form and then joined the Remove itself, leaving in his wake Latin verses composed to celebrate Nelson's victory of the Nile in 1798, slaughtered fauna, and some bruised countenances. His younger brother, William, joined him at Harrow in 1798, thus enabling him to acquire the title 'Temple

6

Senior'. He enthused over Homer and Cervantes, played cricket against Eton, and corresponded with an English boy, Francis Hare, who was living in Bologna. These letters show that the thirteen-year-old Harry possessed some cosmopolitan gastronomic tastes ('when eating nasty things misnamed sausages, [I] envy you at Bologna, who perhaps now are feasting off some nice ones'), and espoused sobriety, telling Hare that 'drinking and swearing . . . though fashionable at present, I think extremely ungentlemanlike; as for getting drunk I can find no pleasure in it.' But he did not agree with Hare's determination never to marry, on account of 'the many faults and vices of women', and replied 'I cannot agree with you about marriage, though I should be by no means precipitate about my choice'.

During the summer vacation of 1799, Harry and his brother William were taken by their father to the House of Commons for the first time. There they shook hands with William Pitt, the prime minister, and sat next to a group of Radical MPs in the members' dining room. Among these members, who were ruminating (with secret relish, so Harry thought) over the recent British military reverses in the Netherlands, was Charles Grey, who in November 1830 was to offer Harry the Foreign Secretaryship in his Whig government.

In the summer of 1800 Temple Senior left Harrow. He had reached the Sixth Form, had messed with Lord Althorp (the future Earl Spencer) and Lord Duncannon, and was considered, according to one observer, to be the best-tempered and pluckiest boy in the school. In his last term he had declaimed with effect on three speech days: first from Tacitus, second from Catiline, and third from Thomas Gray's ode entitled 'The Bard'.

Harry was eventually destined for Cambridge, but that was three years off. Before the outbreak of the French war, the Grand Tour would have helped to fill the gap, but this was now out of the question. Instead, Lord Palmerston decided to send

Harry to Edinburgh University to study the new-fangled subject of Political Economy under the controversial Professor Dugald Stewart, a Radical and a friend of Adam Smith.

So, oddly, the son of the Tory Viscount became a student of a professor accused of Jacobin leanings. Harry eagerly absorbed the academic outpourings of Professor Stewart, who dilated not merely upon the virtues of free trade, but upon the need for a police force, and upon the 'Effects which might be expected on the Morals of the Lower Orders from a Systematical Attention to their Instruction and to their early Habits'. The professor's young and aristocratic disciple filled his notebooks, and remained a lifelong devotee of his tutor's theories of political economy. For his part, Professor Stewart considered Harry's talents to be 'uncommonly good', and even claimed never to have 'seen a more faultless character at his time of life, or one possessed of more amiable dispositions'.

Other pupils of Professor Stewart included Henry Brougham (the future reforming Whig Lord Chancellor), Henry Petty, the son of Lord Lansdowne, and Gilbert Elliot, son of the family friends of the Palmerstons, Lord and Lady Minto. The Mintos, indeed, stayed in the Stewarts' house in Edinburgh where they remarked upon Harry's 'diligence, capacity, total freedom from vice of every sort, quiet and kind disposition, cheerfulness, pleasantness and perfect sweetness'. If anything, the future rip-roaring ladies' man was somewhat staid, and Lady Minto thought there was 'a want of spirits belonging to his age'.

In April 1802 his spirits suffered a heavy blow when his father died of cancer of the throat at the age of sixty-two. The first Harry knew of the crisis was when he was urgently summoned to London to his father's sick-bed. But while Harry was on the Great North Road his father died. By a cruel chance, Harry arrived at Lord Minto's house at Barnet not knowing his father's fate, and there had the bad news casually blurted out to him by a servant who had mistaken him for his friend and travelling-companion Gilbert Elliot. For six weeks Harry was grief-stricken, causing Lord Minto to remark, somewhat unsympathetically, in a letter to his wife that 'He is entirely silent, and at present dejected. He has too little spring for his age; but his heart and disposition, and indeed capacity are good'.

The seventeen-year-old Harry Temple was now the third Viscount Palmerston, with two guardians, the Earls of Malmesbury and Chichester, and Lord Minto to lend him support. Sensibly he returned to Edinburgh to study for his third and final year under the inspired and asthmatic Professor Stewart, of whom it was said there was 'eloquence in his very spitting'.

His time at Edinburgh had a significant bearing upon his later career. His study in 'North Britain' gave him an intellectual capital very different from that acquired by earlier generations who were sent to Italy to become polished gentlemen, yet too frequently returned as dissipated idlers with only a collection of fake antiques to show for their travels. Even in the traditional English universities there was a feeling, brilliantly exposed by Edward Gibbon's *Autobiography,* that hard work was unworthy of a gentleman. At the beginning of the nineteenth century, Oxford and Cambridge were just beginning to emerge from the 'port and prejudice' stage but Edinburgh and Glasgow were the real places to go for new ideas. The Lowlands of Scotland were the heartland of the 'work ethic', a puritanical belief that, rather than being a disagreeable necessity, work is morally uplifting in itself. Few would describe Palmerston as a puritan, yet this aspect of the creed clung to him throughout his life. A great deal of Palmerston's success can be attributed to the fact that he always 'did his homework' very thoroughly indeed.

During the eighteenth century, Scotland had changed from an intellectual backwater into a place of considerable enlightenment. The greatest product of the Scottish Enlightenment was Political Economy. Palmerston was taught that each individual was the best judge of his own interests and thus the government should interfere as little as possible in the lives of its subjects. It followed that anything which hampered the freedom of the individual, particularly in the economic sphere, was reprehensible. Tariff walls and monopoly trading companies, which favoured a small group of producers at the expense of a much larger number of consumers, must be swept away at the earliest possible opportunity. Political Economy had serious implications for social questions. If it was accepted that economic privileges should be viewed with suspicion, it followed that social privileges at least required a justification. Palmerston never doubted the value of an aristocracy; but if the aristocracy was to retain its privileges, it could no longer put up an argument based on a sort of Divine Right. The peers and great landowners had to *show* that they could make themselves genuinely useful and serve the interests of the nation as a whole. Above all else, Political Economy was an empirical creed; its adherents did not care for pious abstractions but demanded action on the basis of statistics and concrete evidence. Would it be possible for Palmerston to square his newly acquired beliefs with the interests of the Tory aristocracy to which his family belonged?

In the summer of 1803, Palmerston left Edinburgh uncontaminated by Jacobinism, and fairly strait-laced into the bargain. In October he entered St John's College, Cambridge. As a nobleman, he was entitled, under an archaic statute, to obtain his MA degree after two years of residence and without the nuisance of having to take any examinations. The young Viscount, however, was not the man to float to his unmerited degree in a riotous atmosphere of gambling debts and drunkenness, like so many of his fellows. He asked to be allowed to sit for the examinations leading to the university's honours degree. This request was not granted, but he sat for his college examinations twice yearly, and twice yearly gained first-class marks. His social life at Cambridge was full but not debauched, and he made it 'a rule always to be in bed by one o'clock, as I am regularly up by seven'. Although he valued 'the habit of mind acquired by preparing for these [twice yearly] examinations', he also remarked judiciously that 'the knowledge thus acquired of details at Cambridge was nothing because it evaporated soon after the examination was over'.

His studies were interrupted in January 1805 by the untimely death of his mother at the age of fifty. Like her late husband, Lady Palmerston died of cancer. Her eldest son mourned her profoundly, but also maturely, telling a friend that 'consolation is impossible: there are losses which nothing can repair; and griefs which time may fix and mellow, but never can obliterate'.

And in Europe there were other things to preoccupy him. The French war had been renewed in May 1803 after the Peace of Amiens fourteen months before. Despite the crushing naval victory at Trafalgar in October 1805, Napoleon's armies were poised on the brink of spectacular triumphs: in January 1806 the military power of Austria was shattered at Austerlitz, and their Russian allies beaten back; in October, the twin battles of Jena and Auerstadt led to the fall of Berlin and the temporary eclipse of Prussia. Though the Grand Army had got no further than Boulogne in the west, it was apparently redrawing the map of Europe in the east with uncomfortable ease.

The prime minister, William Pitt, died in January 1806 with the news of Austerlitz weighing heavily upon him, and amid the collapse of the Third Coalition against France. Pitt's death brought about the resignation of the Tory government and the formation of Lord Grenville's government of the Talents – which brought many prominent Whigs, including Fox, to office; it also produced a by-election at Cambridge where the dead man had held one of the two university seats. Three young noblemen, whose pasts had been curiously intertwined,

competed for the vacant seat: Lord Henry Petty, the radical
Whig candidate, had shared lodgings with Palmerston at
Professor Stewart's house in Edinburgh; Lord Althorp, the
moderate Whig candidate, had messed with Palmerston at
Harrow; Palmerston himself was the third candidate, put up by
the fellows and graduates of St John's to represent the Tory
interest with which his family was traditionally, if rather
unenthusiastically, connected.

The by-election was a curious affair on several counts. For
one thing, two of the contestants held posts in the new
government, Petty being Chancellor of the Exchequer (then not
the prestigious office of the Victorian age) and Althorp was a
Junior Lord of the Treasury; although the sensible thing would
have been for one of them to withdraw, their families belonged
to different Whig factions, and they therefore decided to fight it
out. Another oddity lay in the casual approach of all three
candidates to the election; there were no public meetings (and
indeed they would have served little purpose), merely one letter
from each candidate, and the personal canvassing of the six
hundred or so electors. The contestants managed, furthermore,
to remain on excellent terms and met each other continually.

Palmerston, though undoubtedly anxious to enter political
life, made little impact during the campaign, and was tarred, in
the high noon of abolitionism, with the pro-slave-trade brush –
largely because his father had believed in the maintenance of the
trade. Lord Byron, an eighteen-year-old undergraduate of
Trinity College, Cambridge, dismissed both Petty and
Palmerston in some contemptuous verse:

> Then would I view each rival wight,
> Petty and Palmerston survey,
> Who canvass there, with all their might,
> Against the next elective day.
> One on his power and place depends,
> The other on – the Lord knows what!

The election resulted in 331 votes for Petty, 145 for Althorp, and 128 for Palmerston, hardly a glittering start for one of the most distinguished Parliamentarians of his age.

But Palmerston was nothing if not persistent. In November 1806 the government resigned, two months after the death of Fox, whom Palmerston was willing to acknowledge as among the country's 'illustrious patriots' though earlier 'somewhat infected' (like Wordsworth) with the delirium of the French Revolution. The general election of November found Palmerston standing as one of the two Tory candidates for the double-seated constituency of Horsham. Although Horsham had traditionally been a pocket borough of the Irwin family and Palmerston, after paying out £1500 to Lady Irwin, had their support, the family's pocket developed a serious hole on polling day, and the candidates of the Duke of Norfolk received 44 votes to their opponents' 15. Both sets of candidates, however, considered themselves elected and petitioned Parliament to confirm their election. But when the Commons met in January 1807 the Whigs had a majority, and Palmerston and his partner Fitzharris were unseated.

Grenville's government, early in 1807, passed an Act abolishing the slave-trade and then essayed a measure of emancipation for Catholics, who were still denied important civil rights – such as sitting in Parliament, taking degrees at the universities, or holding commissions in the army and navy. This attempt at Catholic Emancipation ran foul of King George III, who clung fast to his coronation oath, and forced Grenville's administration to resign at the end of March.

The Tories returned to office under the leadership of the Duke of Portland. Almost immediately Palmerston was offered a modest position in the administration as a Junior Lord of the Admiralty. He received the offer as a result of patronage rather than of his persistent, but unsuccessful, performances as a Tory Parliamentary candidate. In Palmerston's own words, the Duke of Portland 'was an old and intimate friend of Lord Malmesbury, who had been one of my guardians. . . . Lord Malmesbury had obtained from the Duke that I should be one of the Junior Lords of the Admiralty.' Palmerston journeyed to London from his estate at Broadlands, dined with his patron, and went to kiss hands for his first office. His fellow Junior Lords consisted of three old sailors, and two minor politicians – one of whom devoted much time to writing novels. Despite the vital importance of sea power to the nation's security, at that time the lay Lords of the Admiralty, according to Palmerston, 'had nothing to do but sign their name'. Palmerston doubtless signed his name as competently as his colleagues, but he still lacked a seat in the House of Commons.

In May 1807 he tried once more for a seat at Cambridge in the general election. The other Tory candidate for the two seats, held by the Whigs Lord Henry Petty and Lord Euston, was Sir Vicary Gibbs, the Attorney General, described as 'quite intolerant and quite sincere'. As polling day approached it became apparent that Euston was almost certain to be re-elected. Gibbs therefore proposed to Palmerston that their only chance of both, or either, being elected was for each man's supporters not to 'plump' for their particular candidate but to bestow one vote on each of the Tory candidates. At the hustings all seemed to be going well until the evening when Gibbs protested that Palmerston's supporters were indeed 'plumping' for him. Brushing aside the advice of his backers, including his tutor Dr Outram, Palmerston urged his people to give their second vote to Gibbs. This honourable intervention cost him a seat in Parliament, for when the votes were counted, Euston had 325, Gibbs 313, Palmerston 310 and Petty 265.

Palmerston's way to the House of Commons was now made smooth by a piece of political juggling. His father had sat for Newport in the Isle of Wight, which was a pocket borough controlled by Sir Leonard Holmes. Sir Leonard was perfectly willing that the young Palmerston should have the seat, but, fearful that the new MP would make an embarrassing bid for local support, stipulated that he 'should never, even for the election, set foot in the place'. Palmerston agreed to these terms. The sitting member was then induced to resign, and Palmerston was returned unopposed. He thus entered Parliament at last with nonchalant ease, and positively forbidden to nurse his constituency, the name of which, in later years, he found it difficult to recall.

The member for Newport took his seat in June 1807. For six weeks he held his tongue and obediently voted with the government, while the French marched over the Pyrenees and Junot's infantry reached Lisbon. But in February 1808 Palmerston made his maiden speech, appropriately enough, in view of his subsequent career, on a great issue of foreign policy. In September 1807 a joint naval and military expedition to Copenhagen had bombarded the city and captured the Danish fleet to prevent it falling into Napoleon's hands. This high-handed demonstration of British resolve antagonised neutral European countries, and gave the Parliamentary opposition a suitable stick with which to beat the government. Canning, on 3 February, defended the Copenhagen expedition in a speech lasting three hours. Late in the evening Palmerston's chance came: he justified the government's refusal to reveal the secret sources which had convinced them that a Napoleonic takeover of the Danish fleet must be pre-empted; he also agreed that proper respect should be paid to 'the law of nations, on right and policy', but qualified this pious opinion by arguing that British interests were paramount to such considerations.

The speech was a successful enough start, and his colleagues warmly congratulated him, even though on opening next morning's papers he found that 'they have not been very liberal in their allowance of report to me'. Still, he sent a fuller account to his sister Elizabeth, to whom he confessed that the experience was not as alarming as he had expected, though he was glad when it was over. His senior colleagues in the government, however, were impressed, and in the summer there was talk of his becoming Under-Secretary at the Foreign Office under Canning.

During the summer recess of 1808 Palmerston went with his brother William to inspect the family's estates in Sligo. His tenants flocked to stare at him, and he quickly saw how desperately the boggy, over-populated land needed reforms. He consequently determined gradually to eliminate the petty landlords, or middlemen, that came between him and his tenants, to introduce a Scottish farmer to supervise agricultural improvements and to build roads, a small manufacturing village and a harbour on Donegal Bay. He also decided to set up three good schools, though he recognised sensibly that the masters would have to 'be Catholics, for the people will not send their children to a Protestant'.

He returned to London for the new session of Parliament, though he made no speeches. His colleagues at the Admiralty noted his capacity for hard work, though socially he was labelled as pedantic, pompous and priggish. In Europe, France was still in the ascendant: Napoleon was in Madrid, and Sir John Moore's force was beaten back to Corunna. In the spring of 1809, Napoleon's decision to concentrate his forces against Austria gave Sir Arthur Wellesley (later Duke of Wellington) the opportunity to begin the slow process of ousting the French from the Iberian peninsula.

With the coming of autumn, the Duke of Portland resigned as prime minister and was succeeded by 'the honest little fellow' Spencer Perceval, formerly Chancellor of the Exchequer. To the general surprise, the new prime minister summoned Palmerston from Broadlands and offered him the now vacant Chancellorship. Palmerston, who was not yet twenty-five, hesitated; he had no great knowledge of finance, and, despite his half-hour maiden speech, did not relish frequent speech-making in the House of Commons; moreover it was widely believed that whoever became Chancellor would be sacrificed as a scapegoat to public dismay over the Walcheren disaster. Perceval, after offering to share some of the burden himself, then proposed to make him Secretary at War.

Palmerston had two days to think it over. He wrote at length to his old guardian Lord Malmesbury, showing how clearly he saw his own limitations. Even though the Chancellorship of the Exchequer was not the choicest plum for an aspiring young politician, it carried onerous responsibilities, especially in wartime, and Palmerston rightly doubted his capacity and experience at that point in his career. So he accepted the post of Secretary at War, though diffidently refusing a seat in the Cabinet. It was a position he was to occupy for the next nineteen years.

2

THE TORY SECRETARY
AT WAR
1809-28

ODDLY, CONSIDERING THAT BRITAIN was plunged deep into an apparently interminable war, Palmerston thought his new post well 'suited to a beginner'. Perhaps he felt comforted by the fact that there was also a Secretary of State for War and the Colonies who was responsible to the Cabinet for the overall policy and direction of the war, thus limiting his own duties to the financial and general administration of the army. Moreover, there was also the Commander-in-Chief who bore the responsibility for military matters such as discipline and promotion. It is also probable that Palmerston, still rather decorous and unassuming, welcomed the opportunities afforded by the War Office for hard and valuable work somewhat removed from the blaze of publicity that from time to time illuminated the more sought-after recesses of, say, the Foreign Office.

Certainly few of Palmerston's contemporaries considered his appointment to be anything more than the product of Lord Malmesbury's influence and of his own aristocratic background. William Huskisson thought it 'a very bad appointment', but Lady Lyttelton mused that 'I suppose we must be glad of it as it may divert his Lordship from flirting, in the same way as people rejoiced at his predecessor's appointment because it was to cure him of gambling'.

When Palmerston first touched his hat to the sentries outside the War Office at the Horse Guards and entered upon his new career, he had close on two hundred staff under him. His salary was £2480 a year, £20 less than that of the permanent head of the department, William Merry. He was soon involved in the routine of his office: he signed his first official letter, dealing with regimental accounts, on 30 October 1809; the next day he committed a guardsman's deranged wife to Bedlam; he grappled day after day with the problems of new issue greatcoats, militia epaulettes, forage, military billets; he corresponded with the Lords Commissioners for His Majesty's Treasury, the Apothecary-General, the Clothing Board, and many others.

His Parliamentary performances were centred on the somewhat arid business of introducing the army estimates to the House of Commons. The estimates were relatively uncontroversial in wartime, and in any case Palmerston spoke on them competently enough, having armed himself more than adequately with the appropriate facts and figures. His first estimates, those for 1810, were faced with some sharp and not always relevant questions from those MPs with service backgrounds: General Tarleton deplored the extravagant folly of the Waggon Train (used for moving supplies) despite Wellington's practical demonstration of its vital importance in the Peninsula War; there were misgivings over the Martello towers, and some hostile queries about the medical services; at one point the prime minister, Spencer Perceval, intervened to help out his young colleague, but two days later the estimates were voted through.

Palmerston's early weeks at the War Office were not entirely devoted to the minutiae of supply, for he soon became embroiled in a heated controversy with the Commander-in-Chief. The occupant of this august, but not always adequately filled, office was Lieutenant-General Sir David Dundas, who had been promoted from Quartermaster-General following the

Duke of York's resignation over the scandal of his mistress, Mrs Clarke, selling army commissions. Dundas had risen from the tradesman's class to become one of Lord Chatham's young eagles during the Seven Years' War of 1756-63; addicted to the drill book, and consequently known as 'Old Pivot', he took issue with Palmerston over the implementation of the 1810 Act of Parliament regulating the supply of regimental clothing. Hitherto the colonel of the regiment had paid the tradesmen for the clothes, and had then deducted the cost from his soldiers' pay; the 1810 Act put the whole business in the hands of the War Office. Without consulting Dundas, Palmerston sent out a circular to this effect, and, at the same time, wrote to all generals asking them for a list of their aide-de-camps in order to ensure that none of them was receiving allowances for fictitious ADCs.

Dundas strongly objected to Palmerston's interference on both counts; though not denying the need to check up on the allowances for ADCs, he insisted that any orders should come from him. He called, moreover, for the repeal of the 1810 Act. The dispute lingered acrimoniously on. Palmerston stuck firmly to what he conceived to be an important administrative principle, that all questions of army finance came within his province; he submitted to the prime minister a lucid 30,000-word document citing 495 cases to prove the independence of the Secretary at War, which office, he argued, acted 'as a sort of barrier between the military authority of the officer in command of the Army and the civil rights of the people'. Before the dispute was referred to the Prince Regent, acting for his incapacitated father George III, Palmerston suffered some embarrassment by the return of the Duke of York to his old position as Commander-in-Chief in May 1811.

On 29 May 1812, as Napoleon stood poised on the borders of Russia, the Prince Regent's order, which merely embodied Perceval's ruling, was issued. It was agreed that the Secretary at War was not subordinate to the Commander-in-Chief, but that the former should not issue any orders to the army without previously submitting them to the latter; in the event of a disagreement, the prime minister would arbitrate between them. Palmerston had shown commendable resolution in the struggle, and had preserved the independence of his office.

At the time it may have seemed no more than an administrative wrangle, but an important constitutional question was at stake, nothing short of the ultimate sovereignty of Parliament. The fact that three different ministers, the Secretary at War, the Secretary for War and the Colonies, and the Secretary of State for the Home Department, had responsibility for some aspects of military affairs meant that the Commander-in-Chief had ample opportunity to divide and rule. It could also be argued that Parliament was far from sovereign when it did not really control the armed forces. The Commander-in-Chief regarded himself as directly responsible to the Prince Regent and certainly not to the Cabinet. The enormous expansion of the Army during the long struggle against Napoleon had allowed Radical scaremongers to talk of a military *coup d'état* with royal backing. It is true that the Regent was often very disparaging about Parliament as an institution but, ultimately, he was too timorous and far too fond of a quiet life to risk supporting such a hazardous move.

In the early nineteenth century, however, the health of many members of the royal family was notoriously poor; it was not out of the question that, one day, the throne would pass to the Regent's brother Ernest, Duke of Cumberland. As King, Cumberland might have had few scruples about calling in the military to stop Parliament from enacting Catholic Emancipation. The problem of control over the Army was not settled finally until after the Crimean War and, of course, the succession of Cumberland is a mere 'might have been'. Palmerston was certainly absolutely correct, however, to resist even a minor encroachment by the C-in-C upon affairs properly handled by a politician. The Secretary at War had demonstrated a remarkable capacity for clear thinking and consistency in argument. Though some of his contemporaries found the controversy a tiresome irrelevancy in the shadow of more stirring events in Europe, Palmerston had in fact served early notice of high administrative competence.

As he proved himself at the War Office, Palmerston also began to prove himself in the drawing-rooms and boudoirs of fashionable society. Though not immediately the most sought-after young man in London, he found no doors closed to him. One important key to social success was membership of Almack's, probably the most exclusive club in the capital. Seven Lady Patronesses governed the club and decided whom to admit to its select membership; among the seven were the Countess Cowper (Emily Lamb), the Countess of Jersey and Madame de Lieven, wife of the Russian ambassador. It is almost certain that each of the three became Palmerston's mistress, and, indeed, Lady Cowper eventually became his wife. At any rate, Palmerston was readily admitted to Almack's, while aspiring applicants from the middle classes were firmly excluded.

Of the three Lady Patrons with whom Palmerston became amorously involved, Lady Cowper was his greatest love. She was born Emily Lamb, a sister of the William Lamb who was destined, as Lord Melbourne, to become Queen Victoria's first Prime Minister. Lady Cowper was beautiful, vivacious, kind-hearted and even-tempered; she was also available. A great many society beaus had affairs with her, and Palmerston was almost certainly the father of her younger children. Her husband, nine years her senior, and with 'a slow pronunciation, slow gait and pace', bore these indiscretions stoically. As for Palmerston, who was already earning the title 'Lord Cupid', he sketched a Cupid for her in her album, and scribbled a verse:

Cease mortals to consume your Prime
In vain attempts at killing Time.
For Time, alas, whate'er you do,
Is sure to end in killing you.

Apart from activities of this sort, Palmerston wrote a few pieces for pro-government journals like the *New Whig Guide* and the *Courier*. He continued his father's friendship with the playwright Sheridan, and together with Sheridan and Canning formed a rather pretentious literary club for the improvement of the English language. The first dinner of the new club was held at Sheridan's house, while the bailiffs were in possession on behalf of the unfortunate man's creditors. Many years afterwards Palmerston was asked whether he and his fellow club members had succeeded in improving the English language, and he replied, 'Not, certainly, at that dinner; for Sheridan got drunk and a good many words of doubtful propriety were used.'

He also spent a good deal of time nursing the university seat at Cambridge, for he was determined to represent that constituency rather than the pocket borough of Newport. His chance came in March 1811 when Lord Euston succeeded to the peerage as Duke of Grafton and vacated his seat. Palmerston at once resigned as MP for Newport, and fought against John Henry Smyth, a nephew of the outgoing member. His assiduous attendance at university and college functions, and the long evenings spent playing whist with dons, paid off, and he was elected by 451 votes to 345. He represented the university until the general election of 1831.

In 1811, therefore, Palmerston could be well contented with his standing. He was MP for his old university, an extremely competent and well-regarded Secretary at War, and a rising star in fashionable circles. Lady Minto, however, still thought him somewhat mediocre: 'Harry is doing very well – with a clear head and a good understanding. He will never be a great man

23

because he has no great views – but he is painstaking and gentlemanlike to the highest degree, and will always swim where greater talents might sink. Nothing can be more amiable.'

Two years later many of Palmerston's fellow-Tories found him less than amiable when he made a rare incursion into non-War Office matters and spoke in the Commons in favour of further measures of Catholic emancipation. Yet Palmerston's support for a Committee to consider emancipation was by no means based upon radical convictions. His philosophy was essentially Tory; he resolutely maintained Parliament's right to impose political liabilities upon any section of the community, yet argued that it was foolish for the state to deny itself the fullest service from Catholic families, who were at present debarred from the highest military offices and altogether from Parliament; what talents would the nation have lost 'if it had unfortunately happened that, by the circumstances of birth and education, a Nelson, a Wellington, a Burke, a Fox or a Pitt, had belonged to this class'? Despite these homely and practical considerations, full Catholic emancipation was still sixteen years off.

In other ways, Palmerston fully approved of the government's policies. He was a staunch supporter of the foreign policy of Lord Castlereagh – that object of Radical scorn and invective – and he apparently remained quite undisturbed by the repressive domestic measures taken by successive administrations in the face of the French and revolutionary threat, such as the Combination Acts and the commonplace political prosecutions for libel and sedition. Nor did the clamour for Parliamentary reform or for the ending of slavery in the Empire move him. Indeed one of his main contributions to the life of Parliament between 1811 and 1815 was his consistent defence of flogging as a means of maintaining discipline in the army.

Palmerston continued to deal briskly and promptly with departmental minutiae, with pay and allowances, while at last the French were driven over the Pyrenees, and, from the east, Russians, Prussians and Austrians converged on Leipzig with the unfamiliar scent of victory in their nostrils. Finally the defeated Napoleon sailed in a British cruiser from Fréjus to Elba, and Europe was, briefly, at peace once more. With the spring of 1815, however, the 'Corsican ogre' slipped from his island exile and sailed for Cannes. As Napoleon marched northwards, France fell once more at his feet:

> *Bon! Bon!*
> *Napoléon*
> *Va rentrer dans sa maison!*

But the Hundred Days ended upon the field at Waterloo, while Brussels listened to the distant thump of the guns, and the War Office enjoyed its Sunday break from routine. Eventually HMS *Northumberland* sailed for St Helena in the South Atlantic, bearing the vanquished Emperor to his last, isolated abode.

In the aftermath of Waterloo, Palmerston efficiently calculated the cost of the 182 battles of the French wars and of the 1812-14 war with the United States. The army had lost 920 officers and 15,214 other ranks killed, of whom almost one-sixth had died in the brief campaign culminating in Waterloo. These were trifling losses compared with the losses of contemporary European powers or, indeed, with British casualties in the two world wars. Still, Palmerston had his own casualties to take care of, and proposed that, in gratitude for the sacrifices at Waterloo, wounded officers should automatically have their pensions increased whenever they were subsequently promoted rather than remain at the level fixed for the rank held when they were wounded. He also suggested that every soldier who had served at Waterloo should be able to count it as equivalent to two years' service for the purpose of pay and pensions.

In August 1815 Palmerston spent five weeks in France, mainly in Paris with the British army of occupation. Since his French was excellent, he was able to gather some accurate impressions of the defeated country. When he landed at Le Havre, for example, he noted that though the white flag of the restored King Louis XVIII flew on all sides, and the customs officials wore white ribbons in their hats, many still regretted the fall of the tricolour, not least a street urchin who sang provocatively:

> Bientôt plus de Guerre
> Tous les Rois sont morts.
> Il n'y a que l'Angleterre
> Qui résiste encore.

He visited France twice more during the next few years, in 1818 and 1821; he met the Duke of Wellington, Tsar Alexander of Russia, and the King of Prussia, watched allied troop manoeuvres, and rejoiced when plundered art treasures were removed from the Louvre. His attitude towards the French had softened somewhat by 1821 when he told his sister Elizabeth, 'With all my predjudice against the French, I must own that there is a great deal of natural good manner and civility among the lower classes, and particularly the women, which one does not meet with in England.'

As Secretary at War in peacetime, Palmerston's task was not an easy one. The annual army estimates came under heavy attack from Radical MPs who wanted a return to a peacetime military establishment. Palmerston resisted these demands, arguing that Britain's new territorial acquisitions overseas, and the excesses and agitations of machine-smashing Luddites and of Radicals at home required the maintenance of a sizeable army. This refusal to cut military spending antagonised members of all political groupings, who blamed the various manifestations of public discontent upon the continuing high level of taxation and upon economic distress. Palmerston was, of course, no reckless spendthrift and in 1821 he tried to pare down the cost of the War Office by reducing all the salaries (except his own) and tightening up on departmental hours and discipline.

He attempted to promote some measure of reform within the army. He advocated army education, on the one hand hoping to turn the habits of the common soldier, who was widely regarded as a red-coated savage, from drunkenness towards enlightenment, and on the other providing the means by which a really professional officer class might be produced. In the latter regard, he was instrumental in wheedling money out of Parliament to set up an officers' college at Sandhurst. He also suggested that if the army established savings banks in which the rank and file could invest a proportion of their pay, and, moreover, if the troops were paid on a more regular basis, it would reduce the all-too-predictable occasions when quite large sums of cash were spent recklessly on drink.

But it should not be supposed that Palmerston in 1820 was an earnest philanthropist and humanitarian. He was still a trenchant supporter of flogging, and notably unsympathetic to individual cases of hardship. Generally speaking, his former diffidence had been transformed into a rather brittle self-confidence, and the amiable, almost inoffensive young man that Lady Minto had discerned in 1811 had become determined, high-handed and abrasive; Lord Cupid, in short, had been superseded by Lord Pumicestone.

Palmerston's rakish deportment was nicely reflected in his dealings with tradesmen. He regularly refused to pay bills, even after repeated, and presumably polite, applications. Between 1811 and 1841 he was sued by his creditors on twenty occasions; in eighteen of these instances judgement with costs was awarded against him, and on one occasion he settled out of court. The sums involved were mostly rather modest, and one creditor was obliged to invoke the majesty of the law to recover a mere £2.12.0 from this obstinate salaried aristocrat with extensive estates in England and Ireland. Of course, Palmerston might have claimed that his duties and obligations as a landlord involved him in a consistently high level of expenditure, and certainly he made a number of improvements to the workmen's cottages, church buildings and schools which stood on his estates – particulary those near Broadlands. He did not overpay his labourers and servants, though he was often reluctant to take harsh measures against his estate farmers who were late with their rents, perhaps believing that his own creditors should show similar forbearance.

Palmerston, the paternalist landlord, was also a rigid believer in the rule of law, and an object of distaste for many Radicals in the years of domestic tumult after 1815. Though Britain did not succumb to the French disease, and the guillotine was not set up at Tyburn, there was enough violence in the air. In 1812 Spencer Perceval, Palmerston's mentor, had been shot dead in the lobby of the House of Commons, and in April 1818 an attack was made upon Palmerston himself. A demented lieutenant on half-pay, called Davies, shot at Palmerston on the staircase of the War Office, but merely grazed his back. The unfortunate man was demonstrably insane, and Palmerston eventually paid for a barrister to defend his attacker in court; Davies was judged to be mad and was committed to Bedlam. In 1820 there was the much more serious revelation that a group of Radicals had planned to murder Cabinet ministers at dinner at Lord Harrowby's house in Grosvenor Square; but the Cato Street conspiracy was foiled and the plotters hanged.

The genuine extent of domestic discontent had earlier been given bloody expression in the 'Peterloo Massacre' of August 1819, when cavalrymen had ridden into the thousands of demonstrating factory workers in St Peter's Fields, Manchester, killing a dozen demonstrators and seriously injuring over five hundred; a number of arrests followed. Palmerston stood staunchly with those who, like the Prince Regent, applauded the tough measures taken at Manchester. He subsequently sought to strengthen the Yeomanry, units of which had played such a conspicuous part at Peterloo, as a reliable, middle-class, counter-revolutionary force. He also asked Parliament in 1820 to grant £70,000 to build barracks for the troops, in the conviction that it was necessary to segregate soldiers from the common populace as much as possible, in order to avoid their becoming contaminated with revolutionary ideas.

Palmerston also steadfastly approved of the controversial Six Acts introduced by Lord Liverpool's government in the panicky aftermath of Peterloo. These Acts, which included the Seditious Meetings Prevention Bill and other measures to restrain the freedom of the press and to suppress sedition and blasphemy, were bitterly attacked by the Opposition in the Commons. But Palmerston, and many of his colleagues, believed that the Acts did not go far enough in their muzzling of the press. He also robustly defended the government's decision in 1820 to enlarge the peacetime standing army to 60,000 claiming that the army was an essential bulwark against attacks on the constitution. He turned on his Radical critics and assailed them with the remarkable proposition that it was misled reformers like themselves, rather than the government, who were threatening military dictatorship, since an extension of the franchise would lead, as history had proved, to a loss of liberty.

Palmerston also became involved at this time in two cases which clearly reflected his unswerving adherence to law and order. One involved the dismissal from the army of General Sir Robert Wilson, who had acquired Radical sympathies and who had been accused of intervening against some units of the army during the civil disturbances that had attended the funeral of Queen Caroline (the estranged and highly controversial wife of George IV) on 14 August 1821. The Opposition took up Wilson's case, but Palmerston insisted that the dismissed general had caused a gross breach of military discipline by encouraging the troops to disobey orders. John Lambton, the future Earl of Durham, known as 'Radical Jack', proceeded to attack Palmerston for his 'sneering' references to Wilson.

The second case, which provided Palmerston's Radical critics with ammunition for a good many years to come, involved a shooting incident on his estate at Broadlands. Poaching was a lucrative but illicit employment for the rural community, and bitter battles were fought between gamekeepers and poachers. In November 1820 a certain labourer called Charles Smith wounded one of Palmerston's assistant gamekeepers in the thigh; he was eventually arrested and sentenced to death under the draconian criminal laws of that epoch. Although there were still 223 offences punishable by death, the sentence was discretionary in nearly all cases, and since 1810 less than ten per cent of those sentenced to death had actually been hanged. Palmerston was badgered with requests to intervene on Smith's behalf; he did so, but only half-heartedly and still trenchantly upholding the justice of the law against attempted murder. Not surprisingly, his two pleas failed, and Smith was hanged. Local feeling was in Smith's favour, and the wounded gamekeeper even collected signatures for a petition to save the convicted man's life; to many important Radicals Palmerston was now stereotyped as a die-hard Tory landlord, an assessment that was something less than fair, but perfectly understandable.

But in 1822 an event occurred which, in its repercussions, was to cause Palmerston a slow, and not always comfortable, realignment of his political sympathies: Lord Castlereagh, the Foreign Secretary whose anti-liberal policies had earned him the fierce hatred of Radicals, and many Whigs, committed suicide. Palmerston, who had approved of Castlereagh's determination to uphold royal despotism in Europe, keenly regretted his loss. Castlereagh's successor at the Foreign Office was George Canning, and his advent brought at least the breeze of change to Whitehall. Canning had progressive views on

30

Catholic emancipation, negro slavery and fiscal protection; he was also little inclined to underwrite foreign tyrants, as his predecessor had done.

Palmerston was sympathetic to the cause of Catholic emancipation, and had absorbed free-trade views while under the tutelage of Professor Stewart at Edinburgh. He also began to espouse the abolition of slavery, and in 1820 had become a discreet, behind-the-scenes, supporter of Wilberforce's Anti-Slavery Society; but in this matter he was a gradualist, arguing that the immediate ending of slavery in the West Indies would bring hardship to white and black alike. However, he thus shared a modest number of convictions with the new Foreign Secretary. In April 1823 Palmerston was also able to give support to Canning in a debate on the recent French invasion of Spain which had crushed the democratic regime and reinstituted an absolutist monarchy; British Radicals demanded that the government should intervene on behalf of Spanish Liberalism. Canning declined to intervene, but told the Commons that if France had Spain, it would be Spain without the Indies; he consequently employed the Royal Navy to thwart the Spanish monarchy's attempts to suppress the independence movements in the Americas, thus calling in the New World to redress the balance of the Old. Palmerston, in his first contribution to a foreign policy debate since his maiden speech, refused to compare the recent French invasion with Napoleon's earlier assault, and argued that to have given the Spanish Liberals false hopes of British support would have been a cowardly act. The phrases he used in this debate were striking enough, and provided a foretaste of things to come: 'To have talked of war and to have meant neutrality, to have threatened an army and to have retreated behind a state paper, to have brandished the sword of defiance in the hour of deliberation and to have ended with a penful of protests on the day of battle would have been the conduct of a cowardly bully.'

In fact, Palmerston was moving towards a Canningite position. The Tory party was in process of dividing into a Canningite, or progressive, group and a reactionary faction that clustered round the Lord Chancellor, the unbending Lord Eldon. Palmerston did not identify with these progressive Tories straight away – indeed he still remained steadfastly unprogressive on a number of issues. Nonetheless, the year or so following Canning's accession to the Foreign Office show Palmerston considering change of one sort or another. In 1822 he was offered the post of Governor-General of the East India Company's territory in India, but he declined this chance of exercising a quasi-royal sway over a distant subcontinent. In 1823 he even contemplated marriage to Lady Georgiana Fane, the daughter of the Earl of Westmorland, and the younger sister of Palmerston's mistress Lady Jersey; but Georgiana refused him, twice as it happened, and he remained enmeshed with Lady Cowper.

But change was nonetheless in the air. There was some angry criticism of one of the phenomena of the age, 'this infernal nuisance – the loco-motive Monster, carrying *eighty tons* of goods and navigated by a tail of smoke and sulphur, coming thro' every man's grounds between Manchester and Liverpool'. Ministers like Huskisson at the Board of Trade were itching to lay disrespectful hands upon the system of fiscal protection, and the free-trade wind was blowing strong. Meanwhile at Ascot, Prinny, who had some time ago staggered the world of fashion by 'letting down his belly', strutted as His Britannic Majesty King George IV in a black cravat and wig, with a plain brown hat tilted over one eye, and with Lady Conyngham in tow 'hardly visible but by her feathers'.

In 1826 there was a general election which produced the remarkable sight of Palmerston returned as a member for Cambridge University on the votes of Canningites and Whigs. It had been Palmerston's record on Catholic emancipation that had drummed up this support, and he acknowledged, with perhaps an air of surprise, that 'the Whigs have behaved most handsomely to me, they have given me cordial and hearty support, and, in fact, bring me in'. He showed considerable impatience with the Tory party, 'that stupid old Tory party, who bawl out the memory and praises of Pitt while they are opposing all the measures and principles which he held most important'. Nor were his leaders spared his scorn, from 'old women like the Chancellor (Robinson), spoonies like Liverpool, ignoramuses like Westmorland, old stumped-up Tories like Bathurst'. Above all he recognised that:

On the Catholic question; on the principles of commerce; on the corn laws; on the settlement of the currency; on the laws regulating the trade in money; on colonial slavery; on the game laws, which are intimately connected with the moral habits of the people; on all these questions, and everything like them, the Government will find support from the Whigs and resistance from their self-denominated friends.

In February 1827, it seemed as if the Canningites' day had come, for the prime minister, Lord Liverpool, suffered a stroke and resigned. After some weeks of manoeuvring, Canning became prime minister and was promptly deserted by Tories like the Duke of Wellington, Lord Eldon (inevitably) and (less inevitably) by Robert Peel; but William Huskisson, Palmerston, Lord Dudley and Charles Grant stayed with Canning, who even brought William Lamb and other right-wing Whigs into his administration.

In forming his government, Canning offered Palmerston the Chancellorship of the Exchequer, though more out of gratitude for his support than from any high regard for his qualities. Canning indeed considered that Palmerston had reached the 'summit of mediocrity'; he was, moreover, embarrassed by the latter's indirect involvement in a financial scandal of the Devon and Cornwall Mining Company. Palmerston, however, refused the Chancellorship at this point, since his accession to a new post would have necessitated his standing for re-election at Cambridge, which he considered too inconvenient. But it was agreed that when the new Parliamentary session opened he would than take up the Chancellorship.

As it happened, Canning did not honour this understanding, and instead offered Palmerston the Governorship of Jamaica. Palmerston apparently laughed at the very notion, and a little later also refused the post of Governor-General of India. Both these offers give the impression that if Canning was not trying to kick Palmerston 'upstairs' he was at least trying to kick him to the colonies instead. At any rate, Palmerston stayed on as Secretary at War, though with a seat in the Cabinet. But Canning was ailing, and died in August 1827, five months after becoming prime minister. His place was taken briefly by Lord Goderich, who was in turn dismissed by George IV in January 1828.

The Duke of Wellington was now invited to form a ministry. The Canningites bargained with the new prime minister and, assured that Catholic emancipation would remain an open question and that Canning's foreign policy would be adhered to, agreed to serve under him. Palmerston seems to have felt few qualms at having deserted his new Whig allies for Wellington, arguing that the latter would provide a strong but reasonably liberal government. Wellington's government, however, was soon bitterly at odds over issues like the struggle for Greek independence from Turkey, the introduction of free trade, and the approach to Catholic emancipation. Palmerston was a steadfast supporter of Canningite principles in Cabinet, and opposed Wellington so determinedly that the prime minister came to dislike him keenly.

Finally, Palmerston and Huskisson quarrelled with Wellington over the redistribution of two grossly underpopulated Parliamentary constituencies, which they favoured giving to the new urban conglomerations of Birmingham and Manchester.

The Iron Duke spoke of 'mutiny'; Huskisson resigned; Palmerston tried, and failed, to save him, and in May 1828 he and other leading Canningites resigned their posts. After nineteen years at the War Office, Palmerston took up an unfamiliar place upon the back benches.

Of course, Palmerston liked being in office. The fact that the Tories had enjoyed a virtual monopoly of power since 1783 was a strong reason for shunning any arrangement with Grey. Palmerston was not a rich man – Irish estates were notoriously unremunerative – but, more important, he liked the feeling that he really could influence events. His failure to resign earlier, however, was not mere opportunism; there were many obstacles to his joining the Whigs. In the past the Whigs had opposed the continuation of the war against Napoleon, an attitude which to Palmerston seemed little short of treason. They had resisted measures like Sidmouth's Six Acts which in Palmerston's view were essential to preserve the country from revolution and anarchy. Even now, he was well aware that it is much easier to indulge in progressive generalisations in opposition than in government. Even admitting their good intentions, the Whigs had been out of office too long. Grey and Althorp seemed only gentlemanly amateurs, lacking the vital professional expertise to enable them to govern efficiently.

This charge could not be made against the experienced Tories who had enacted a number of valuable practical reforms in the 1820s. So long as Canning lived, there was a chance that the Tories would be the party of technocrats, the party which understood the needs of business better than the Whigs ever could. It could be a party which decided its policy on pragmatic grounds without too much reference to the ideology of either Right or Left. Unfortunately, the balance between progressives and die-hards could no longer be maintained. Wellington's accession to power seemed to indicate that the die-hards had won. Palmerston came to the conclusion that the Tory opposition to Catholic emancipation or to any change in Parliamentary representation was based on stupid humbug. Lord Eldon was solemnly protesting that the main obstacle to the admission of Roman Catholics to Parliament was that it would involve the King breaking his sacred coronation oath and would thereby endanger His Majesty's immortal soul – a view shared by both George III and George IV. The Edinburgh rationalist and materialist was bound to react against nonsense like that.

Ultimately Wellington was forced to grant Catholic emancipation, but there were reasons of interest in determining Palmerston's drift towards the Whigs. It was clear that the Tory heir apparent was the Home Secretary, Robert Peel, as hard working, more experienced and much more respectable than Palmerston; if Palmerston had ideas of a great career, particularly if he thought of the premiership, then Peel would be an enormous obstacle if he remained within the Tory party. Peel was prepared to swallow a lot of his party's obscurantism that Palmerston found unacceptable, but, like Palmerston, Peel was fundamentally a technocrat whose mission to modernise the Tory party came to grief in 1846. Palmerston was probably wise to get out when he did.

The great attraction of the Whigs was that men of Palmerston's experience in government were almost non-existent. If Palmerston put himself up for sale, Grey would probably be forced to pay a high price. Such speculations would be a waste of time if the Whigs were never given the chance of office. George IV had made it clear that he would never accept Grey as Premier but, by the middle of 1828, it was obvious that the King was a very sick man. The Duke of Clarence was a Canningite Tory in outlook but had no personal grudge against Grey. When George IV died, Whig chances of success would rise sharply.

3

THE WHIG
FOREIGN SECRETARY
1830-4

PALMERSTON spent two years without office. They were not, however unprofitable years. Away from the statistical and financial shuffling of the War Office, he began to concentrate upon foreign policy – an appropriate enough commitment for a disciple of Canning. Though by no means able to dazzle the House of Commons with oratorical fireworks, he developed an effective style of delivery, peppered with robust phrases. Moreover, his subject-matter was far more likely to catch the public attention than deft answers to questions on the Maltese Fencibles or on pay-warrants to officers serving in the Channel Islands.

On 1 June 1829 he made a speech on foreign policy which bathed him in the bright light of an unaccustomed, but not unwelcome, publicity. Palmerston in fact gave his public reputation ample opportunity to blossom by ensuring that his speech was printed and copies sent to Hansard, fellow-MPs and newspapers, an early indication of how he was prepared to manipulate the existing means of communication. He attacked the government's policy towards Portugal and Greece in aggressive and assertive terms, and at the same time banged the drum of constitutional liberty – to the evident satisfaction of the Whigs. On the Portuguese question, Palmerston criticised the

Wellington government for its failure to adequately protect certain subjects who had suffered ill-treatment at the hands of Dom Miguel's absolutist regime. He claimed that 'Buonaparte in the plenitude of his power never treated the humble representatives of a petty German principality with more contemptuous disregard than that which our remonstrances have met with at the hands of Dom Miguel'. As for the argument that Britain was not entitled to interfere in the internal affairs of other nations, Palmerston replied:

If by interference is meant interference by force of arms, such interference, the government are right in saying, general principles and our own practice forbade us to exert. But if by interference is meant intermeddling, and intermeddling in every way, and to every extent, short of actual military force; then I must affirm that there is nothing in such interference which the laws of nations may not in certain cases permit.

He went on to criticise Wellington's support for a truncated Greece 'which would contain neither Athens, nor Thebes, nor Marathon, nor Salamis, nor Platae, nor Thermopylae, nor Missolonghi'. He concluded by claiming that, under Canning, Britain had been the friend of liberty, but that now she apparently conceived 'her advantage to lie in withholding from other countries that constitutional liberty which she herself enjoys'. On 10 March 1830 he made another speech on the subject of Portugal in which he praised Liberalism and denounced the dastardly Dom Miguel.

Why did Palmerston decide to concentrate his considerable energies upon foreign affairs at this point in his career? An orthodox and pious explanation would be that he was determined both to emulate Canning and to serve his country in an area vital to its continuing supremacy. But Palmerston was no high-minded, sober idealist; he was a supreme opportunist, who developed to a fine art the ability to mould and to be attuned to public opinion. There are consequently practical reasons why he plumped for foreign affairs: one was that he was pleased and impressed with the public response to his first speeches on foreign policy, and no doubt it was a welcome change from struggling to get the army estimates through the Commons; another reason lay in his linguistic abilities: he could, after all, speak excellent French and Italian, and he was never one to waste a personal advantage – whether with the ladies or with political opponents; he was, moreover, in opposition (never something he much cared for) and he probably considered that the government could be harried effectively over foreign policy and, in the process, weakened, thus opening the way for his own return to office. Of course, it is also possible that he simply accepted the office because Grey (who may well have wanted an inexperienced and dependent political convert in the post) offered it to him.

At any rate, to broaden his experience of Europe he travelled to France in January 1829 to see things at first hand, returning for a second visit towards the end of the year. He went to the court of the last Bourbon King, Charles x, attended a public lecture of the historian and future chief minister Guizot, dined with Polignac, and went the round of *soirées*. He found the French 'Ultras' to be grotesque replicas of die-hard Tories, and fancied that, judging from the mood in Paris, there might soon be 'a change of name in the inhabitant of the Tuileries, and the Duke of Orleans might be invited to step over from the Palais Royal'. In July 1830 his surmise was vindicated and a revolution in Paris brought Louis Philippe, Duke of Orleans, to the French throne as that novelty (for the time) the 'Citizen King'.

Palmerston wholeheartedly approved of the Liberal constitutionalist revolution of July 1830, and indeed he now espoused Liberal causes with a verve that would have appalled the novice Secretary at War twenty years before. As a man who rarely did things by halves, he was now prepared to exult that 'We shall drink the cause of Liberalism all over the world'. He also invariably voted with the Opposition in favour of giving the seats from rotten boroughs to the new urban areas of the North and Midlands.

All that remained was for the Whigs to come in and for Palmerston and other Canningites to join the new Cabinet. The opportunity came in June 1830. The King died at Windsor, nearly blind, and 'very nervous but very brave' in the face of death; there would be no more strutting in peacock clothes, no more raffish parties in the Pavilion at Brighton. A general election automatically followed the death of the monarch; as a consequence the Whigs were much strengthened in the House of Commons. The Duke of Wellington did not resign, but rather sought to lure the Canningites into the government; Palmerston resisted his blandishments, but left room for negotiation. Then in the autumn the slow-footed Huskisson was knocked down by a steam locomotive at the opening of the Liverpool-Manchester line and fatally injured; the death of the most pro-Tory of the leading Canningites removed an important bridge between that group and Wellington.

It became clear towards the end of 1830 that the new King, the pineapple-headed William IV, would have to send for Lord Grey and ask him to form a Whig administration. Palmerston's name was mooted as Foreign Secretary, though Grey initially preferred Lord Lansdowne (Palmerston's friend Henry Petty during his Edinburgh days). Madame de Lieven, the intelligent and scheming wife of the Russian ambassador, commended him strongly to Grey, to whom she was very close; her advocacy of Palmerston for the Foreign Office may have owed something to the fact that they had almost certainly been lovers at one time, but it is more likely that she was satisfied that he would bring pro-Russian sentiments to the post. Grey may also have been influenced by the arguments that in any Whig government that contained a substantial number of Radicals, the presence of

Palmerston at the Foreign Office would reassure those foreign régimes which harkened back to the days of Castlereagh; for though Palmerston in 1830 thought of himself as a Canningite prepared to cooperate with the Whigs, he had no great love for Radicals, and many suspected that, in his bones, he remained a Tory.

At any rate, when in November 1830 Wellington's government was defeated in the Commons on Henry Brougham's resolution for a substantial measure of Parliamentary reform, the King sent for Grey, and Grey, in turn, sent for Palmerston whom he considered to be sufficiently inexperienced in foreign affairs to be a pliable subordinate. Palmerston thus became Foreign Secretary at the age of forty-six; it was not an office he had hankered after and few expected him to make a success of it.

During his first days at the Foreign Office Palmerston complained, fairly light-heartedly, that he was 'like a man who has plumped into a mill-race, scarcely able by all his kicking and plunging to keep his head above water'. As Foreign Secretary he was obliged to work extraordinarily hard, either at his desk or attending debates in the Commons. Even during Parliamentary recesses he stayed in town attending to his dispatches. He was only able to visit Broadlands infrequently, until the opening of a convenient railway line in 1847 made the journey easier for him.

Because he committed himself to such grinding toil, Palmerston expected his subordinates at the Foreign Office to work hard too. He soon made himself unpopular by clamping down on his clerks, ensuring that they worked proper hours, did not indulge in horseplay, and ceased to flirt with the girl dressmakers in Fludyer Street at the back of the Foreign Office building in Downing Street. He also forbade his clerks to smoke, reduced their salaries and coal allowance in 1841 in the interests of economy, urged them to write in black ink in a clear, bold hand, and often kept them at their desks until ten o'clock at night. Palmerston vetted their grammar, scanned their drafts for words of an unbecoming foreign origin, and insisted that their sentences be economical and to the point. If a clerk or diplomatic representative violated Palmerston's standards in these matters he reacted censoriously, but also sometimes humorously; thus on one occasion he wrote on a letter in his own beautiful script, 'Has the Writer of this Letter lost the use of his right hand? If not, why does he make all his letters slope backwards like the raking masts of an American Schooner?'

The routine of Palmerston's day, though flexible, was demanding. His daily desk-work required eight hours' work, then there was attendance at the House of Commons or at official functions. He tried never to go to bed later than one o'clock in the morning, and never to rise after seven o'clock. Even when he had been obliged to sit late in the Commons, he still got up at seven o'clock, took some exercise (riding when he was in London), read some dispatches, and then took breakfast. He arrived at the Foreign Office at 10 am, and worked solidly through till the early afternoon; instead of a midday meal he ate an orange; Cabinet meetings were held in the afternoon, but were generally over by 5 pm; between five o'clock and 6.30 he was available to ambassadors and other callers on business. He then ate his one large meal of the day; this was understandably a sizeable repast, and even in the last year of his life he was capable of consuming a huge amount:

. . . he ate two plates of turtle soup; he was then served very amply to cod and oyster sauce; he then took a pâté; afterwards he was helped to two very greasy-looking entrées; he then despatched a plate of roast mutton (two slices) . . . there then appeared before him the largest, and to my mind the hardest slice of ham that ever figured on the table of a nobleman, yet it disappeared just in time to answer the inquiry of the butler, 'Snipe, or pheasant, my lord?' He instantly replied 'Pheasant', thus completing his ninth dish of meat at that meal.

Palmerston finished off with pudding, jelly, dressed oranges, and half a large pear. After his evening meal he went down to the House of Commons, going home as soon as he was able. He then worked at his dispatches until 1 am, preferring to stand at a special desk for fear of falling asleep.

Of course, he still found time for some pleasurable activities. Although he was in his late forties when he became Foreign Secretary, he still cut a dashing, youthful figure, was always fashionably dressed and sported luxurious side-whiskers. The Tory press, particularly *The Times,* continued to refer to him as 'Lord Cupid', and played up the image of the dissolute, middle-aged rake. In fact, although Palmerston undoubtedly pursued a number of women, in addition to Lady Cowper, with varying degrees of success (Lady Jersey did not resist him, but the young Catholic widow Mrs Petre probably did) his colossal work-load as Foreign Secretary gave him little time for prolonged dalliance.

Palmerston insisted on drafting all important departmental dispatches himself, and left only trivial matters in the hands of his Under-Secretaries. He also wrote numerous articles for the press (often in the same words as his dispatches), and several newspapers, the *Observer,* the *Courier,* the *Morning Chronicle* and the *Globe* followed editorial lines that he had laid down in return for payment out of the Secret-Service money; this was not exactly bribery, rather the buying of government 'advertising space'. Although Palmerston oiled the printing-presses of some journals with Secret-Service money he did not personally supervise this body, whose main function during this time was not wholesale and intricate espionage on the scale of the modern MI5, but rather occasional payments to British firms abroad who had bought secret information.

Palmerston soon developed a reputation for arrogance and plain speaking during his lengthy tenure of the Foreign Office. Certainly he was not inclined to be deferential, or even polite, as a matter of course, though he generally treated other aristocrats courteously enough. But even when communicating with an aristocratic ambassador abroad he sometimes wrote letters to which, in the words of Lord Ponsonby, no man could submit.

His lack of condescension also found expression in his capacity to keep important visitors waiting, and in his unpunctuality. There was often a queue outside Palmerston's door at the Foreign Office, and foreign diplomats who expected more considerate treatment were sometimes outraged: Talleyrand, the French Foreign Minister, was not infrequently kept waiting between one and two hours for an interview, and once the Corsican-born Russian ambassador Pozzo di Borgo, after a two-hour wait outside Palmerston's door, complained bitterly of the Foreign Secretary's insolence. He was also notorious for late arrivals at banquets and dinner-parties, and it was said that he always 'missed the soup' on these occasions. He showed little remorse for this behaviour, and usually gave the perfunctory excuse that he had been detained on official business. Since, in fact, his official routine ran in an efficient and well-regulated way, this excuse wore a trifle thin, and the probable explanation of his conduct is that he simply did not care what society thought of him.

Much the same can be said of his attitude towards foreign states. From his appointment as Foreign Secretary in 1830, Palmerston became increasingly identified with the more forthright (even brash) opinions entertained by a large section of the nation. In some respects, of course, the expression of his own political prejudices and patriotism did much to foster such opinions. The techniques which Palmerston employed in the conduct of foreign affairs were perhaps not new, but they were nevertheless startling. They included a bluntness and sharpness of tone that was sometimes spiced with condescension.

Palmerston believed that foreigners in general would do well to listen to British advice and to respect British achievements. He had a particularly low opinion of foreign absolutists, and developed a frank distrust of France and Russia. This led him on occasion into undiplomatic utterances, even bluster. Bulwer indeed said of him, 'generally when Lord Palmerston talks of diplomacy, he also talks of ships of war'. Although the great powers of Europe might shrug off such verbal assaults, lesser powers might consider that they were being bullied.

The plain fact was that Palmerston was vigorously dedicated to the promotion of British interests. This sometimes led him into liberal policies, and sometimes into illiberal ones. This is not to deny Palmerston's sympathy for Liberal movements abroad, but it does partly explain why he occasionally pursued courses which seemed offensive and selfish. Even when, in 1840, for example, Palmerston dispatched the fleet to Naples to threaten a despotic regime that he openly disliked, the main motive behind the move was to ensure that the Neapolitan government did not contravene their 1816 commercial treaty with Britain. On other occasions, Palmerston actively supported illiberal causes – like that of the Southern Confederacy in the American Civil War.

His view of the nature of Britain's interests was neatly expressed when he announced in 1843 that 'the sun never sets on the interests of this country'. The vast expansion of Britain's industries, her world-wide web of commercial activity, made a global supervision necessary. Although, in general, peace could be equated with prosperity, resolute intervention in a dozen small trouble-spots was an acceptable corollary of this peace. Palmerston summed it up when he said, 'Diplomats and protocols are very good things, but there are no better peace-keepers than well-appointed three-deckers.'

Palmerston had, after all, been born and bred in the years when a succession of crushing British naval victories over the French, the Spaniards and the Dutch had saved Britain from invasion, contained Bonaparte's ambitions, and secured the country's interests in the Atlantic and the Mediterranean, and in

India and the East. It thus seemed natural to him to use the fleet with a resolution not far removed from the activities of Nelson or Jervis.

He was not, however, dedicated to the extension of the Empire. What Britain held he was prepared to defend, but to paint the map wantonly red, or to rashly extend dominion over untutored savages, would have seemed to him an irrelevance. This was chiefly because he tended to view the Empire according to business principles. To be saddled with unprofitable territories that were merely a drain on the resources of the British government would have appalled him. In this respect he was very much a man of his times, and by the late 1850s the system of economic protection that had bound Britain and her colonies together for two centuries had been dismantled; free trade prospered in its place.

Palmerston, the conservative Whig, had in fact much in common with the Cobdenites. But while he opposed the irresponsible acquisition of further territory, he was also determined to prevent European rivals from laying their hands on strategically desirable or profitable colonies. French interest in New Zealand and Tahiti was snuffed out; the Russians were put in their place in Chinese waters. France's ambitions in Morocco were sharply curtailed because 'Her Majesty's Government wish that the Empire of Morocco should exist according to its present limits'. Palmerston did not deny that many parts of the world would be better governed by Britain (or even by France), but he also preferred to 'try to improve all these countries by the general influence of our commerce . . . let us all abstain from a crusade of conquest'.

His foreign policy was, therefore, essentially pragmatic and consistently self-interested. He had no blue-print to stick to, except the preservation of the status quo in the international balance of power, and his means of pursuing this object were necessarily flexible and opportunist. He did not generally dispatch the gunboats unless diplomatic means of resolving problems had first been exhausted. Nor did he invent 'gunboat diplomacy', of which British and French history provide dramatic earlier examples. It was merely that the strength of the Royal Navy could be readily utilised as a means of enforcing British foreign policy, and Palmerston, with the British public behind him, was prepared to utilise it.

Palmerston's abilities were put quickly to the test when he first became Foreign Secretary. In 1830, in the wake of the French revolution of July, the Belgian people had also risen in revolt and had proclaimed their independence from the King of Holland who had ruled jointly over the Dutch and the Belgians since the 1815 Peace of Vienna. France announced her determination to support the Belgians, but Prussia was prepared to back the King of Holland in a campaign of reconquest; Austria and Russia, fearful of European revolution, supported Prussia. But Metternich, the Austrian Chancellor and Foreign Minister, did not relish war, and the British government, led by Wellington, pressed for an international conference on the Belgian question. This conference began meeting in London shortly before Wellington's government fell and Palmerston took over at the Foreign Office.

As chairman of the conference, Palmerston was thus plunged headlong into an international crisis within forty-eight hours of taking office. He immediately advocated the policy favoured by the outgoing government, that Belgium should become an independent and neutral state. Although admitting that the union between Holland and Belgium had been in 'the interest of both England and Prussia', he recognised that the Belgian revolt nullified such hopes in practice. What he wanted above all was to prevent France incorporating Belgium within her own frontiers.

The drawing of the boundaries of the new state gave the London conference the most trouble. Palmerston maintained throughout that this was a matter for the great powers to decide, and that both the Belgians and the Dutch should keep out of the discussions. But although the principle of Belgian independence was agreed by the conference on 20 January 1831, the final treaty was not ratified by the great powers until the middle of 1832. In the interim Palmerston strove to prevent France from taking over Belgium; this was particularly difficult since French troops invaded the country in August 1831 to counter an earlier Dutch invasion. Palmerston was ceaselessly engaged in diplomatic activity during the Belgian crisis: he had to deal with Leopold, the newly-elected King of the Belgians, with Talleyrand and Metternich, with Prince Lieven for Russia, Baron Bülow for Prussia and many others; he had to wrestle with the complex problems of the frontier fortresses, free navigation on the Scheldt, the Belgian national debt, and the future status of Luxembourg and Limburg. He was in turn stubborn, tactful, subtle and threatening.

On the point of the treaty's acceptance, the Belgians instructed their plenipotentiary Van de Weyer to refuse to sign it because they were obliged to evacuate Eastern Luxembourg and Limburg. It is symptomatic of Palmerston's persuasiveness and persistence that he managed to overbear Van de Weyer, reporting that 'I have been at [him] all yesterday and today have persuaded him that the only use of a plenipotentiary is to disobey his instructions, and that a clerk or messenger would do, if it is only necessary strictly to follow them . . . the patient Van de Weyer [is] in the adjoining room waiting to know his fate and scratching out and altering just as we tell him to do.' Despite subsequent Belgian objections, Van de Weyer's alterations stood, though the King of Holland refused to accept the treaty.

Palmerston was soon faced with other problems further afield than Belgium. In February 1831 there were revolts in Italy in the Papal states and in the absolutist provinces of Parma and

Modena. Metternich, determined to thwart revolution in Italy, which Austria considered her sphere of influence, sent in troops to Bologna, while the French government, somewhat unwillingly, occupied the Papal port of Ancona on the Adriatic as a counter-move. Palmerston had a much weaker hand to play in Italy than in Belgium, though he strove manfully to persuade Austria and France to settle their differences peacefully. But short of contemplating a full-scale (and unacceptably expensive) exercise of Britain's armed strength, there was little that he could effectively do. Nonetheless he urged Metternich to use his influence to moderate Papal revenge as the Liberal movement collapsed and to induce the Pope to grant modest constitutional concessions to his subjects; he also withdrew Seymour, the British representative in Rome, since his continuing presence at the Papal Court might be interpreted as underwriting the policy of repression. But Palmerston's entreaties were not acted upon, and by the end of 1832, though Austria had withdrawn from Bologna and France from Ancona, the Italian revolutionary movements had been crushed.

If Palmerston had little real opportunity to alter events in Italy, he had still less chance of effectively aiding the cause of Liberalism in Poland following the revolt of November 1830. The Poles in that part of Poland ruled by Russia rose against the repressive régime of the new Tsar Nicholas I. The French were prepared to support the revolutionaries, but the Russians steadily reconquered the insurgent areas, destroyed all traces of constitutional liberty and incorporated Poland into Russia, which was contrary to the provisions of the Peace of Vienna. Palmerston's attitude to this crisis was essentially pragmatic: he sympathised with the Poles' desire for constitutional freedom, but disapproved of the extremist Radical flavour of the revolt; moreover, he did not want to antagonise Russia when he needed her goodwill during the Belgian crisis. His policy was also inevitably dictated by national self-interest, and he said: 'Now the English nation is able to make war, but it will do so where its own interests are concerned. We are a simple and practical nation, a commercial nation; we do not go in for chivalrous enterprises, or fight for others as the French do.'

While Continental Liberals and revolutionaries struggled for greater constitutional liberties, the British nation was convulsed with the crisis over the Reform Bill. The Whig government had pledged itself to improve the Parliamentary franchise and to redistribute Parliamentary seats, and in March 1831 Lord John Russell introduced a Reform Bill. The Bill was a modest enough affair by later standards, providing for the redistribution of 168 pocket and rotten boroughs and the enfranchisement of some thousands of chiefly middle-class males. This Bill passed through the Commons by one vote at its second reading, but was subsequently defeated in committee. The prime minister, Lord Grey, then asked for a dissolution of Parliament; at the ensuing general election on May 1831 the electorate, fearful of violent revolution, voted in the Whigs with a greatly enlarged majority.

Palmerston had done well by changing sides; his new position was much more influential and prestigious than that of the Secretary at War. Yet there are some indications that Palmerston's first years with the Whigs were not happy. He was essentially a man of the Centre who had abandoned the Tory party because it was too obscurantist; would he now find that his new allies were equally unacceptable? Palmerston had been in favour of a redistribution of seats but he was certainly taken aback by Lord John Russell's Reform Bill. The Foreign Secretary was less enthusiastic for 'The Bill, the whole Bill and nothing but the Bill' than other members of the Cabinet. Abstract notions of 'The Rights of Man', propounded by some of the government's more extreme supporters, were leading to demands for annual parliaments, universal suffrage and the ballot. Palmerston found the dogmatism of the Left as repellent as the obscurantism of the Right. In particular, he was alarmed by the strategy of men like Ellice, Durham and Brougham who believed that the only way to pass the Bill was to stir up feeling 'out of doors' and use popular anger to intimidate the Tories, the House of Lords and even the King himself. Palmerston was inclined to support proposals for compromise but, for the moment, his influence was small compared to that of the hot-heads.

Palmerston lost his seat at Cambridge in May 1831, coming bottom of the poll, and had to find another seat at Blechingley in Surrey – ironically a constituency due for disenfranchisement under the Reform Bill. Palmerston stood on the right of the Cabinet during the Reform Bill crisis, together with Lord Melbourne and the Duke of Richmond; but the left, led by Lord Althorp and Lord (Radical Jack) Durham, dominated government attitudes, for behind them, it was felt, were the nation's Radical, revolutionary forces which would brook no opposition.

Though Palmerston would have preferred a Bill based on a compromise with the Tories and the House of Lords, he was prepared in the spring of 1832 to propose to William IV that if the Lords threw out the now modified Bill then the monarch should create enough Whig peers to swamp the Tories in the upper house. The King refused to do this, the government resigned, Wellington held the premiership perilously for nine days then was forced to resign in the face of financial panic and the possibility of revolution. William IV then agreed to create new Whig peers, the House of Lords gave way under the threat and the Reform Bill was passed. Palmerston had throughout remained unenthusiastic for reform, but had predictably found it expedient to accede to popular clamour. In any event, the provisions of the Bill were hardly revolutionary, and there was little chance that British Jacobins would now sit in serried ranks on the benches of the House of Commons.

The passing of the 1832 Reform Bill affected Palmerston's foreign policy, since the hostility of the Continental despots to the measure and the enthusiasm of Continental Liberals for the supposed 'English Revolution' made it necessary to give firmer support to Liberal movements in Europe. Thus in August 1832 he openly supported the cause of constitutional progress in Germany, and declared 'Constitutional states I consider to be the natural allies of this country'. He subsequently sent a dispatch to the President of the German Diet (the forum for members of the German Confederation) deploring the repressive Six Resolutions passed earlier in the year.

The Foreign Secretary's support for liberal movements on the Continent reduced – but by no means eliminated – the antagonism towards Palmerston displayed by many sections of the Whig party. The early 1830s were years of economic difficulty and it was widely believed that prosperity would only return if taxation was drastically reduced. Not all of the Radicals were internationally minded. Men like Joseph Hume believed that charity began at home, and feared that a forceful foreign policy would be used as an excuse to increase taxation – which still fell more on the poor man than on the rich. Palmerston's style, too, disturbed many on his own side. He was even more remote and arrogant to backbench Whigs than he was to the representatives of foreign governments. Edward Ellice, the Chief Whip, constantly complained that the Foreign Secretary appeared not to know more than half-a-dozen ordinary members, he never took any of them into his confidence and, indeed, the Tories seemed to know more of the government's future plans than its own supporters did. Palmerston was not the man to suffer fools gladly and would not waste time cultivating people who were mere lobby fodder. Perhaps Palmerston did have better things to do, but it was a failing which had serious consequences.

Palmerston's relations with the aristocratic section of the

Whig party were not much better. Reservations about lack of professional expertise amongst the Whigs which had worried Palmerston in the 1820s proved to by fully justified. Long years in opposition had made the great Whig magnates hungry for office. When Grey came to power, they believed they were entitled to their reward for years of profitless devotion. They clamoured for appointments in the diplomatic service for themselves and for their relations. Palmerston refused point blank to give key embassies to men with virtually no diplomatic experience. If Britain was to be properly represented, there was no alternative to the promotion of essentially Tory career-diplomats. The decision to put the interests of the country above those of the party was very commendable and underlines Palmerston's technocratic approach to government: but the choice of Tories like Howard de Walden as Ambassador to Portugal and Lord Ponsonby to the Ottoman Empire infuriated the Russells and Hollands who had impecunious relations to provide for.

All these complaints provided the ammunition for Palmerston's enemies within the Cabinet. Grey's government was an ill-assorted coalition which, once it had passed its Reform Bill, could agree on virtually nothing else. It just could not pull together as a team. Grey was becoming a very cantankerous elderly man, Melbourne was good humoured but idle, Althorp was more interested in his estates than in being Chancellor of the Exchequer, Durham was intolerably conceited and much given to tantrums, Ellice was false and slippery and there were well-founded doubts about the sanity of Brougham, the Lord Chancellor. Altogether it must have been a very trying experience for Palmerston. Almost everyone was trying to do down his colleagues and Ellice was beginning a campaign to eject Palmerston from the Foreign Office and replace him with Durham. In such a back-biting atmosphere Palmerston was forced to develop his links with the press to rebut the allegations made against him in journals controlled by his enemies. Promising young men like Stanley and Graham left the government in disgust and eventually joined the Tories. There must have been times when Palmerston regretted ever leaving the Tories but there could be no going back now. Peel, Wellington and Aberdeen reviled Palmerston as the arch apostate, whilst the attitudes of his present colleagues ranged from distrust to hatred. In 1833 and 1834 the political future of Viscount Palmerston must have looked precarious in the extreme.

Soon events in the Near East pushed Palmerston towards hostility with Russia. The Tsar intervened in support of the Turkish Sultan against his rebellious subject, the Viceroy of Egypt, Mehemet Ali. In payment for his action against Mehemet Ali, Nicholas extracted from the Sultan the Treaty of Unkiar Skelessi, which promised cooperation and mutual aid and was signed in July 1833; of utmost danger to British interests was a secret clause that allowed Russian warships to enter the Dardanelles (which gave access to the eastern Mediterranean from the Black Sea) in peacetime, though the warships of other powers could not. Palmerston eventually protested most vigorously against the Treaty of Unkiar Skelessi, thus antagonising the Russian government and pushing Russia towards the Müchengrätz declaration of October 1833 when Austria, Prussia and Russia declared their united opposition to revolution.

As a counterblast to this thinly disguised revival of the notorious 'Holy Alliance' of absolutist powers after 1815, Palmerston rigged up the Quadruple Alliance in Western Europe. The Quadruple Alliance was signed in April 1834; it bound Britian and France to support the Liberal-inclined governments of Spain and Portugal against reactionary Pretenders. It was hailed as a great triumph for Liberalism, and Palmerston wrote 'I should like to see Metternich's face when he reads our treaty'.

Thus, almost without meaning to, Palmerston had emerged by 1834 as the accredited champion of constitutional freedom throughout Europe. It is a sufficient indication of the apparent metamorphosis he had undergone that when, in November 1834, the Whig government, which had since June been led by Lord Melbourne, was dismissed by the antagonistic William IV, Palmerston wrote to the British chargé d'affaires in Vienna that he should 'tell this immediately to Metternich, it will gladden his heart and be the most agreeable thing he has ever heard from me'. Metternich, the alleged apostle of reaction, did not apparently exult, but as Palmerston left the Foreign Office after his first four-year stint his clerks unashamedly rejoiced that their hard taskmaster had gone. Their celebrations, however, were somewhat premature, for in five months' time he was back.

4

BULLY TO THE
WEAK?

1835-46

IN JANUARY 1835 the Tory government led by Sir Robert Peel fought a general election in an attempt to gain a majority in the House of Commons. This they failed to do, and after dragging out a few more miserable months as prime minister, Peel resigned. So the Whigs were back and William IV accepted them 'as a good child swallows a dose; quickly, though with some wry faces'; the languid Lord Melbourne became prime minister, and his less languid sister Lady Cowper was once more well placed to advance the cause of her lover Palmerston.

Palmerston had failed to win a seat at the January election despite some resolute canvassing and the presence of his friend Admiral Osmaney, who was to act as second if the candidate should become involved in a duel. When Melbourne formed his administration in April and, after spurning the Colonial Office and assorted Governorships Palmerston once more became Foreign Secretary, he still lacked a constituency. Such problems were, however, not insoluble given ready cash; Palmerston paid the Whig MP for Tiverton £2000 to resign his seat, and in June was returned unopposed for that constituency.

When Palmerston returned to the Foreign Office events in the Iberian peninsula were to occupy much of his attention. Although the Portuguese civil war had ended by 1835 and

Queen Maria da Gloria was apparently settled on the throne, British interests there had to be carefully maintained. Palmerston considered Portugal to be a country where British influence could be vigorously exploited, and his deportment towards the Portuguese government was frequently assertive and insolent. An excellent example of his methods can be found in the question of the marriage of Queen Maria. In May 1835 Palmerston sniffed out the fact that negotiations were taking place concerning a possible match between Maria and the Duke of Nemours, son of Louis Philippe of France. He was opposed to the prospect of a closer connexion between Portugal and France, and his diplomatic pressures, which included the threat of ending the ancient Anglo-Portuguese treaties, snuffed out the marriage negotiations. After this triumph he went on to press the claims of Prince Ferdinand of Saxe-Coburg-Gotha as consort to Queen Maria; it is a remarkable reflection of British influence that, despite the objections of some of the Portuguese ministers, Ferdinand married Maria in April 1836.

Between 1835 and 1840, however, further difficulties with Portugal arose. The Portuguese government continued to allow the slave-trade - mainly to their ex-colony of Brazil. Britain was the scourge of the international slave-trade, and the ships of the Royal Navy claimed the right of search of foreign ships suspected of slaving - but only if the right was granted by the foreign government. There was, however, no such treaty between Britain and Portugal. Palmerston, though no great enthusiast for the abolition of slavery throughout the British Empire in 1833, was zealous in his activities against the slave-trade, and he consequently tried to bully the Portuguese government into granting Britain the right of search.

He also badgered Portugal to drop its tariffs against British goods, and in addition insisted that if British subjects in Portugal were brought to trial they should face a jury composed half of Britons and half of Portuguese. Moreover, he waged a persistent and ruthless campaign to exact from the Portuguese authorities any debts or compensation owed to British citizens. Eventually in March 1840 he sent a note to the Portuguese government (now composed of right-wing Liberals) telling them that unless they paid all their debts at once Britain would seize Portugal's colonies. This peremptory note was not, in fact, delivered by the British diplomatic representative in Lisbon, and a somewhat milder communication (though containing veiled threats) followed. Palmerston proceeded to mix a few sparse concessions with his belligerency, and by May 1840 an agreement had been reached.

Spain simultaneously proved a much thornier problem for British foreign policy. The civil war between the right-wing supporters of Don Carlos and the Liberal supporters of Queen Isabella posed severe difficulties for Palmerston. He was anxious that Isabella's government should triumph, yet reluctant to spend British money to that end, and at the same time determined that France, a more trenchant supporter of the Isabellinos, should not exert undue influence in Spain. He summed up his policy in a speech in the Commons when he declared that 'the object was that for the future there should be neither an Austrian Spain nor a French Spain, but a Spain that should be Spanish'. He remained steadfast to that principle even when, in October 1840, Queen Isabella fled to France and General Esparto became Regent with extreme Radical backing. For Palmerston the important points remained the exclusion of excessive French influence and the settlement of Spanish debts. When he resigned as Foreign Secretary in August 1841 he could be satisfied on the first score, though less so on the latter.

While these spectacular events were being played out in Iberia, Britain acquired a new sovereign. In June 1837 Princess Victoria, daughter of the Duke of Kent, ascended the throne, and was soon entranced by the worldly-wise Lord Melbourne and by her Foreign Secretary. She found Palmerston 'a clever and agreeable man . . . so very clear in what he says', and laughed at his jokes till her gums showed. In view of the depths to which Palmerston's reputation was later to sink in Victoria's eyes, the first year or so of their official relationship was little short of idyllic. The young Queen plied him with a wide assortment of questions – many of them exceedingly trivial: she took his advice on chess tactics, consulted him over dinner lists, and was pleased when 'he rode near on the other side for some little time and admired Tartar very much'. For his part Palmerston went to enormous pains to explain to his sovereign the meaning of the word 'bureaucratic', and on another occasion informed her that the Duke of Lucca should be invited to a function 'by note instead of by card. Your Majesty may think this is a small matter, but the Duke is a small Sovereign'. At the same time the Queen noted that her Foreign Secretary 'was a little apt to sneer sometimes and to make it appear absurd what people said'.

Still, she remained devoted to her Whig government, and during 1839 she watched the voting in the House of Commons with an anxious eye: 'we had a majority of 22 . . . delightful and feel that I can breath again. Thank God!' A little later the young Queen noted 'We had only a majority of 5! This struck to my heart and I feel dreadfully anxious!' But in May 1839 Melbourne felt obliged to resign and the Queen, via the Duke of Wellington, sent for Sir Robert Peel. However, Peel was no Melbourne, and Victoria complained: 'the Queen don't like his manner after – oh! how different, how dreadfully different, to that frank, open, natural and most kind, warm manner of Lord Melbourne'. Fearing isolation in this cold and threatening political environment, Victoria refused to exchange her Whig Ladies of the Bedchamber for Tory equivalents; a constitutional crisis swirled through their petticoats, and after the taking of much advice (not all of it impartial), the Queen had her Whig ministers back again. Palmerston was thus still master of foreign affairs, which was satisfying enough in view of his opinion that 'I don't at all conceal that I think it a great bore to go out; I like power, I think power very pleasant'.

He had other causes for satisfaction in 1839, notably his belated marriage to Lady Cowper. Her husband, of whom Palmerston was strangely fond, had died two years before, on the second day of the new reign, but she did not immediately fling herself into Palmerston's arms. Palmerston persisted with his proposals, however, and his de facto brother-in-law, Lord Melbourne, was touched by the 'excessive niceness of his steady perseverance' and told his sister that 'if she like it, to do it, not to potter about it'. By October the pottering was over, and two months later the fifty-two-year-old bride married the fifty-five-year-old groom at St George's, Hanover Square.

The Palmerstons' wedding was not the only one to note in 1839. William Ewart Gladstone had married in the summer, and a few months afterwards Benjamin Disraeli took a willing widow to the altar. Even the young Queen was poised on the brink of matrimony, having succumbed to the charms of an upright young German prince, Albert of Saxe-Coburg-Gotha, who flourished a faint moustache and a 'slight but very slight' pair of side-whiskers. Victoria took a keen interest in Palmerston's wooing of Lady Cowper, though unsure whether late marriages were apt to be successful, and wrote to Albert, 'The *Second,* as you always called Palmerston, is to be married within a few days to Lady Cowper, the sister of my *Primus* . . . . They are, both of them, above fifty, and I think they are quite right so to act, because Palmerston, since the death of his sisters, is quite alone in the world . . . still, I feel sure it will make you smile'.

So Palmerston drove down under winter skies to Broadlands with his bride. There, in the lee of the New Forest, they spent their honeymoon, which could have contained few surprises for either of them. At least Broadlands, with its rather severe paved hall, its Reynolds's, its billiard table and racing trophies, now had a mistress. Christmas passed, and the New Year, and Lady Palmerston was able contentedly to tell a friend that 'Lord P. is utterly and entirely devoted to me and so completely happy that it is quite a pleasure to look at him'.

Lady Palmerston was for her part devoted to her husband and to his political interests. She was soon giving parties from their new town house at 5 Carlton Terrace that were much talked of in society. Early in 1840 her brother Melbourne thought she looked uncommonly well in 'rather a dashing gown', and the Queen also observed that she was now dressing better. His marriage gave Palmerston a domestic anchor that he had lacked before, even though he continued to sail in other waters from time to time.

While Palmerston was reordering his domestic circumstances his foreign policy was unfolding vigorously. As he waited for Lady Cowper's 'yes', an army of Britons and sepoys struck into the heart of Afghanistan on an ill-fated mission to destroy Russian influence there; simultaneously British commercial interests were leading to the Chinese Opium War, while in 1840 he dispatched the fleet to Naples to break the régime's sulphur monopoly and to protect British merchants.

The Afghan invasion, though urged on Britain by the Governor-General of the East India Company's territories, Lord Auckland, commended itself to Palmerston as a means of purging Afghanistan of Russian influence. Palmerston wished to keep Russia on the other side of the Himalayas, and states to the north-west of British India friendly to British interests. But the Afghan invasion was miscalculated: there was no Russian influence to stamp out at Kabul, and a large part of the East India Company's forces were eventually forced to retreat through the snow-filled Khyber pass and were massacred almost to the last man. Palmerston came in for his share of criticism for this disaster, and in particular for his editing of the published dispatches of Alexander Burnes, the British envoy in Kabul, who had been murdered by the mob before the catastrophic retreat. There is no doubt that Palmerston did cut passages out of Burnes's dispatches that proved that the government in important respects acted against his advice, and the bitter criticisms evoked by his forgeries lingered on until his death.

The Naples sulphur crisis of 1837-40, on the other hand, saw Palmerston rapturously applauded by Radicals and foreign Liberals. In 1837 the government of Naples granted a monopoly in the Neapolitan sulphur mines to a cartel dominated by the exiled members of the French Bourbon family. Palmerston claimed that this grant violated Britain's most-favoured-nation position under the commercial treaty of 1816. He proceeded to demand that the recent monopoly grant be rescinded and that British merchants who had suffered financial loss as a result of the monopoly should receive compensation. Failing to find satisfaction, he sent the fleet to Naples in April 1840 with instructions to blockade the port and to seize Neapolitan shipping.

The tyrannical régime of Ferdinand, King of Naples, was thoroughly hated by Radical opinion in Britain; Palmerston was thus able to appear as the champion of the oppressed while being in fact chiefly concerned with the interests of British commerce and British subjects. The crisis was resolved through the mediation of the French government; Palmerston largely got his way, and the subjects of King Ferdinand were abandoned once more to the oppressions of their autocratic state. The sending of the fleet to Naples was perhaps mainly significant as one of the first occasions when Palmerston actually used force in Europe since becoming Foreign Secretary – the first being the Royal Navy's blockade of the Scheldt and Rotterdam in 1833.

Force was, however, used further afield in order to smash

open the door to the lucrative trade of the Chinese Empire. Conflict between the bustling, thrusting British merchants on the China coast and the formal, stultified and arrogant Chinese government was made more likely by the difficulty in establishing recognisable diplomatic relations. To the Chinese the British, and indeed all Europeans, were barbarians, and some recent British ambassadorial forays had foundered on the Chinese insistence on humiliating deportment, including kow-towing. The Opium War which began at the end of 1839 arose from the effort of Commissioner Lin Tse-sü at Canton to stamp out the illicit, but hitherto accepted, trade in opium. The drug was brought from India and exchanged for Chinese tea; it provided one of the most profitable areas of external trade for the British East India Company. A long and tangled sequence of events, involving Chinese charges of piracy and smuggling, culminated in an action between ships of the Royal Navy and Commissioner Lin's war junks, four of which were sunk.

The military balance between early-Victorian Britain and the antiquated forces of the Celestial Empire was ludicrously tilted against the Chinese. Despite China's enormous population, and its ancient history and culture, the technological achievements of Britain gave her an irresistible military advantage; determined hunters, bearing new weapons, had come at last to mutilate and cow the stiff-jointed dragon. Palmerston took a strong line on the terms to be extracted from the Chinese authorities, brushing aside the protests of the young William Gladstone against 'this unjust, this iniquitous war'. He demanded full compensation for opium confiscated from British merchants, the cession of an island off the China coast, the repayment of debts owing to British traders, open trade with the ports of Amoy, Foochow, Ningpo, Singapore and Canton, and that the Chinese should pay the cost of the British military and naval operations against them! He wrote: 'the British Government fervently hopes that the wisdom and spirit of

Justice for which the Emperor is famed in all parts of the World, will lead the Chinese Government to see the equity of the foregoing demands'. This appeal to reason was doubtless less effective than the power of the Royal Navy's guns, and when the Treaty of Nanking was concluded in August 1842, even though Palmerston was out of office it was his terms that were settled upon – even though he took little joy in the cession of Hong Kong, whch he had dismissed as 'a barren Island with hardly a House upon it'. His lack of enthusiasm for Hong Kong, though misplaced, was perfectly understandable; Palmerston wanted the extension of British commerce rather than the extension of the British Empire, and in the case of the Opium War he pursued his objective with steely single-mindedness.

More complex and infinitely more risky than the assault on the Celestial Empire was the protracted international crisis surrounding Mehemet Ali fron 1839-40. The military success and independence of the rebellious Viceroy of Egypt threatened the stability of the Middle East (called the Near East by contemporaries) and the Eastern Mediterranean. This geographical area was particularly important to Britian because of the short overland route to India. As long as the Turkish Empire exercised an effective control over the Near East and the Eastern Mediterranean, British strategic and commercial interests were not threatened, and the encroaching power of Russia (which was simultaneously pushing menacingly eastward into Central Asia) could be contained. But Britain's policy of preserving the status quo was obviously threatened by Mehemet Ali's challenge to the authority of the Turkish Sultan.

In 1839 the Sultan made a desperate bid to curb Mehemet Ali's power by ousting his son Ibrahim from Syria; Russia ominously declared support for the Sultan, and the Turkish fleet deserted to Mehemet Ali and sailed to Alexandria. There was now a real possibility that Ibrahim would march on Constantinople and thus provoke a full-scale Russian intervention – something which both Britain and France were anxious to avoid. Both powers consequently sent a combined fleet to the Dardanelles, which had the effect of giving Russia pause. At the same time, Palmerston proposed that a conference of the five great European powers (Britain, France, Russia, Prussia and Austria) should consider the problem. He also supplied his own diplomatic formula for solving the crisis: Mehemet Ali's forces should abandon Syria in return for the recognition of their leader as hereditary Pasha of Egypt. There were some difficulties in implementing this bargain: one was that Mehemet Ali could not be driven from Syria by Turkish arms, and it was therefore expecting a great deal of him to withdraw voluntarily; the other was that Mehemet Ali was already the de facto hereditary ruler of Egypt.

Palmerston persisted, however, in his attempt to oust Mehemet Ali from Syria. He swept aside the argument that Mehemet Ali's régime was efficient though autocratic, and insisted that 'I hate Mehemet Ali, whom I consider as nothing better than an ignorant barbarian . . . I look upon his boasted civilisation of Egypt as the arrantest humbug'. Though Mehemet Ali, in fact, compared very well with Sultan Mahmud II, the point was that Palmerston believed that British interests could be more effectively asserted if the ramshackle Ottoman Empire remained the dominant power in the Near East. His plans, however, were brought to the point of ruin in July 1839 when Mahmud II died, and his ministers received the shattering news of the rout of Turkish arms in Syria. The Ottoman government therefore proposed to confirm Mehemet Ali as Viceroy of Syria, and were only forestalled by Metternich's suggestion (via the great powers' Conference in Vienna) that the settlement of the Syrian problem should be left to the five powers. The Turkish government then decided not to send their offer to Mehemet Ali.

As the crisis subsided in July, with Mehemet Ali anxious not to antagonise the great powers further, Palmerston's solution to the problem remained fundamentally the same, namely that Mehemet Ali must be driven out of Syria – preferably by the five powers acting in concert. But there was considerable sympathy for Mehemet Ali in France, where it was hoped that the promotion of French interests in the Levant would flow from an alliance or understanding with the Viceroy of Egypt. Palmerston disapproved of these aspirations but was still hopeful of preserving the Anglo-French alliance.

By the middle of 1840, however, Palmerston had become convinced that Britain and the Northern powers (Russia, Prussia and Austria) must move against Mehemet Ali without French cooperation. He threatened Melbourne with his resignation if the Cabinet insisted on obstructing this policy, and argued that unless his advice was acted upon the result would be 'the practical division of the Turkish Empire into two separate and independent states, whereof one will be the dependency of France, and the other a satellite of Russia; and in both of which our political influence will be annulled, and our commercial interests will be sacrificed'. Melbourne and the Cabinet gave way, and Palmerston was able to get the ambassadors of Russia, Prussia, Austria and Turkey to agree to the Treaty of London in July 1840. The Treaty contained a series of ultimatums to Mehemet Ali the mildest of which proposed to confirm him as hereditary Pasha of Egypt and as Viceroy of Southern Syria for life, and the severest of which threatened to remove his Egyptian viceroyalty from him.

The French government was outraged at the Treaty of London; there was some hysterical talk of an Anglo-French war, and all Europe stirred uneasily. Palmerston had calculated that France would not risk war: 'France now is a very different thing from the France of the empire. Then war was the only way which anybody had of getting money; now war would put an end to most people's chance of getting money. A quarter of a century of peace does not pass over a nation in vain.' He remained unperturbed throughout the summer and autumn of 1840, and cooly instructed the British chargé d'affaires in Paris to convey 'in the most friendly and inoffensive manner possible that if France throws down the gauntlet, we shall not refuse to pick it up; and that if she begins a war, she will to a certainty lose her ships, colonies and commerce before she sees the end of it; that her army of Algiers will cease to give her anxiety, and that Mehemet Ali will just be chucked into the Nile'.

The Cabinet still took a less phlegmatic view than Palmerston; Lord John Russell in particular talked of resignation and Victoria wrote to Melbourne that 'the Queen really could not go through that *now*, it might make her *seriously ill* . . . she has had already so much lately in the distressing illness of her poor Aunt to harass her.' British Radical opinion, for less private reasons, deplored the breach with France and the bid to cast down Mehemet Ali in alliance with the despotic Northern powers; on the other hand, Palmerston received some hearty and by no means accustomed support from the Tories.

The Near Eastern crisis of 1840 in a sense solved itself during the autumn. The Syrians rose in effective revolt against Ibrahim, the British fleet took Beirut and Acre, and Mehemet Ali's forces fled for home as best they could. The fleet then sailed to Alexandria, where the Admiral, Charles Napier, negotiated an agreement with the personally charming and astute Viceroy of Egypt. After much international diplomatic haggling, Mehemet Ali was confirmed as hereditary Viceroy of Egypt in the summer of 1841.

Palmerston had won a tricky game hands down. The integrity of the Ottoman Empire had been maintained; the Russians had not gained excessive influence in Constantinople; the French had not gone to war; Britain had not become entangled in any lasting and embarrassing alliance with the Northern powers, and in July 1841 the five powers signed a convention which stipulated that no foreign warships should enter the Dardanelles while Turkey was at peace – thus denying Russia the advantages of the 1833 Treaty of Unkiar Skelessi.

Palmerston had now been at the Foreign Office for ten years and his success was in sharp contrast to the generally dismal record of Melbourne's government. The Foreign Secretary's position was still precarious. It is certainly true that, as Melbourne's brother-in-law, Palmerston was better placed in the struggle for power than he had been under Grey, but dislike of the Foreign Secretary had only increased with the passing years. If Palmerston put a foot wrong his chances of survival would be small. Melbourne liked him personally but the prime minister was too indolent to have done much on his behalf if he had got into serious difficulties.

Palmerston's enemies thought their day had come with the Eastern crisis, when a strong case could be made against the Foreign Secretary's policy. By 1840, partly because of the Great Reform Bill, English people enjoyed greater freedom than the peoples of other lands. Many believed that it was the duty of the British government, particularly a Whig government, to help the cause of freedom elsewhere. After England, the most liberal régime in Europe was that of Orleanist France. In promoting the cause of freedom, therefore, England and France should stick together; they had a common interest against the absolutist régimes of Austria, Prussia and Russia. Much of Palmerston's earlier foreign policy, particularly his support for the independence of Belgium and his backing of the constitutionalist cause in Spain and Portugal, was entirely consistent with this analysis.

Over the Eastern crisis Palmerston was performing an outrageous diplomatic somersault which made many question whether he had ever been a genuine Liberal at all. Life under Austrian rule, which Palmerston had often denounced as intolerable, compared very favourably to the sometimes brutal tyranny of the Ottoman Empire. Yet Palmerston was seeking to preserve a heathen theocracy whose monstrous treatment of its Christian subjects had induced the Foreign Secretary himself to be a fervent advocate of Greek independence in the 1820s. Mehemet Ali, originally an Albanian tobacco dealer, might not be an ideal ruler but, at least compared to the Sultan, he stood for progress. In order to achieve his dubious objective Palmerston was apparently prepared to throw in his lot with the absolutist powers of Europe and deliberately antagonise the only other liberal country. It seemed obvious to Ellice, Holland and Russell that the Orleanist regime was the best Britain could hope for in France. If Palmerston succeeded in ejecting Mehemet Ali from Syria he would be humiliating France. If the Orleanists were disgraced then there was a good chance of popular fury toppling Louis Philippe; the red bonnets would be out again, the guillotine at work and revolutionary armies marching all over Europe. Palmerston would be responsible for this catastrophe!

Of course, men like Ellice were prepared to seize on anything in order to discredit Palmerston. Ellice went to Paris at the height of the crisis and – according to Palmerston – actually urged the French Premier, Thiers, to stand firm. Ellice believed that such a stand would strengthen those who opposed the Foreign Secretary in England. Thus, if Palmerston's ideals were a little tarnished, the behaviour of his enemies was even more unscrupulous. On the face of it, it is difficult to square Palmerston's support of the constitutional cause in Western Europe with his hostility to Mehemet Ali in Egypt. But Palmerston's motto was 'Britain First'; although he was temperamentally in favour of the constitutionalist cause, there were other considerations. Palmerston supported the liberals in Belgium, Spain and Portugal because he thought that long term forces made a liberal victory inevitable and also that such régimes would be good for British exports.

In the Near East the issue was more clouded. In any case, the cultural background for a genuinely constitutional government in Egypt was extremely feeble. Unlike Ellice and his friends, Palmerston was well informed. He knew the size and likely effectiveness of the military forces involved. He had enough information to know that the Sultan could gain at least a temporary respite. He knew too that France was far less friendly to Britain than the Francophiles believed and also that any weakening of the Ottoman power was bound to benefit Russia whose presence on the northern borders of India was already causing concern. French prestige did suffer and although the Orleanist régime lasted for another seven years, its reputation for a timorous foreign policy certainly contributed to its downfall. In 1848 Palmerston may have wondered if he had been right.

While Palmerston stood firm during the Near East crisis, cowed Neapolitans, and humbled the Chinese, he also asserted British interests against the United States of America. The young republic was not, however, easy to bully and overawe; indeed in two wars, the War of Independence and the War of 1812-14, it had inflicted signal defeats upon Britain. Palmerston did what he could all the same. He refused to back down over the border disputes between the United States and British North America, and even went so far as to remove an embarrassingly unfavourable map (which had been drawn up during the Anglo-American peace negotiations of 1793) from the British Museum to the security of the Foreign Office.

There were also squabbles with the United States over the right of search of ships suspected of slave-running, and over the facilities sometimes afforded to escaping slaves in Canada and the British West Indies. More immediately threatening than such long-standing disputes, however, was the Macleod case of 1840-1. Macleod was arrested in New York after he had claimed, while drunk, to have been one of the Canadian militiamen who had burned the American steamboat the

Caroline on the Niagara river, killing one American, during the 1837 Canadian Rebellion. Macleod had in fact merely been guilty of whisky talk, and had been nowhere near the *Caroline* on the night in question. Nonetheless, in New York plans went forward to try him for murder. Opinion on both sides of the Atlantic was inflamed, though the United States government wished to secure Macleod's release. Palmerston took up the prisoner's case with vigour, and let the American Minister in London know 'speaking not officially, but as a private friend, that if Macleod is executed there must be war'. In the event of the execution Palmerston planned to withdraw the British representative in Washington and to send the fleet to the United States coast. Although he was out of office when the Macleod case eventually came before the courts, his strong line had its effect; the American government was anxious to avoid a showdown and Macleod was acquitted and smuggled over the Canadian border.

When, in August 1841, Melbourne's government resigned, having previously seen the Tories win a majority of over a hundred seats in the general election of June, Palmerston's public reputation stood high, and his handling of the Near Eastern crisis had even moved Disraeli to compare him favourably with the elder Pitt in the columns of *The Times.* But there was now more to Palmerston than the diplomatic and bureaucratic scourge of foreign potentates, for during the election of 1841 he had used his campaigning at Tiverton to emerge as a demagogic nationalist leader with keen sympathies for the oppressed and the poor. Doubtless Chartist heckling and Radical criticism helped him move with the times, but whatever the cause he now attacked French atrocities in Algeria, supported the new Poor Law, and flayed the slave-traders. It was all a far cry from the days of the young Tory 'Lord Cupid'.

By 1841 there could be no doubt of Palmerston's importance. His hard work and constant application had meant that he was now more knowledgeable about foreign affairs than any other politician. Of course, he had taken risks; but it is important to appreciate that these were *calculated* risks and that is why they were so uniformly successful. The Foreign Secretary's signal victory over Mehemet Ali and his French backers had enormously enhanced Palmerston's reputation in England. Aggressive patriotism had been somewhat muted since the end of the Napoleonic Wars. Post-war depression, the Reform crisis and the social upheavals of industrialisation had all deflected attention away from foreign affairs. It was some years before Palmerston's message got through. By 1841, however, there was a growing pride in being British, a feeling that the country was unique, more prosperous and more powerful than other nations. Britain's achievements had been enormous and her very success was seen as an indication of divine approval. It followed that Britain had the right and the duty to take a more active role in world affairs. In such a climate, Palmerston's stock was bound to rise.

Palmerston's views on foreign questions and his powerful patriotism reached a much wider public than the audience in the public galleries at Westminster. He had established close links with *The Globe* newspaper in the days when his position was threatened by Durham. Now he used the same medium to defend his policy in the Near East. Palmerston was one of the first Cabinet ministers to make a careful study of the arts of propaganda and to appeal to the public as a whole over the heads of the political establishment. The invention of the steam press and now the development of a national railway network meant that it was possible to increase the production of London newspapers, and, not many years later, it would be possible to deliver them on the day of issue to towns in the Midlands and the North. Palmerston was fortunate that although he had no direct influence over the Tory-inclined *Times,* that newspaper was increasingly sympathetic to him. The *Morning Chronicle,* the organ of the anti-Palmerston forces in the Whig party, was in considerable financial difficulties.

The Foreign Secretary frequently wrote editorials for *The Globe*. The style was rather more snappy than the ponderous sentences of *The Times;* there was even an occasional joke or innuendo to retain the reader's interest. Palmerston knew that if one was to get an idea over to the public, it really had to be hammered in. Day after day *The Globe* declared that those who opposed Palmerston's policies were motivated only by spite and envy, yet they had gone to the very brink of treason to achieve their aims. Palmerston, by contrast, was selflessly working day and night to serve the nation. He knew best; he was always right.

By the end of 1840 the attempt to get Palmerston out of the Foreign Office had collapsed. There was simply no alternative. Despite later recognition of its importance, Durham's mission to Canada was regarded as a fiasco by contemporaries. Lord Holland had died suddenly and the credibility of Edward Ellice was utterly destroyed. Melbourne and Russell, who had not been keen on Palmerston's policy to begin with, quickly came round to support it when it became obvious that it was going to succeed. In previous elections, Whig party managers had regarded Palmerston almost as a liability; now it was clear that Palmerston was a major vote winner. The Foreign Secretary was beginning to move up into the small circle of men who could be considered potential premiers. Melbourne's health was not good; Lord John Russell enjoyed greater prestige in the party but Palmerston was certainly the most popular figure with the ordinary man.

Palmerston was elected for Tiverton in 1841, but the national election results removed the Whigs from office. At least he now had a more settled domestic life to sustain him while in opposition. He and Lady Palmerston were perfectly happy together, and when his wife was obliged to spend some days away from him she wrote 'It is idle of the housemaids to leave your windows open and fire out, and you should send and scold them for it, for it might give you a very bad cold after coming from your warm sitting-room'. And a little later she chided him amiably enough: 'I am so glad to think you had an amusing dinner yes[terday], instead of passing your evening all alone. How glad L[ad]y J[ersey] will have been to get hold of you without me . . . . But what a vile Man to go to bed early now and get up early – to give the world an *impression* that it is *I* who lead you astray – however, notwithstanding this, I am glad to think you should have an early night, for the sake of your eyes.'

Both Palmerston and Lady Palmerston remained attractive individuals as he reached his late and she her mid-fifties. She was still able to roll a brilliant and coquettish eye, and he remained as trim and sprightly as ever – a living advertisement for hard work and regular exercise. Palmerston continued to be an enterprising ladies' man, and in 1839 had shocked the young Queen's sensibilities by attempting to seduce one of her Ladies-in-Waiting at Winsdor Castle. Owing to the still persuasive advocacy of Lord Melbourne, Palmerston's misdemeanour was overlooked, but more than a decade later Prince Albert revived it in an attempt to get him dismissed from office.

Apart from matters of the heart, there were plenty of other diversions. Palmerston hunted regularly with the Hursley Hunt and the New Forest Foxhounds, shot on his Broadlands estate, rode often and walked briskly. He was also a substantial race-horse owner, and his horses won the Cesarewitch in 1841 and the Ascot Stakes in 1853; in 1845 he was elected an honorary member of the Jockey Club. The Palmerstons moreover travelled quite extensively during the opposition years of 1841-6: to see his slate quarry in Wales, to the family estates in Sligo, and to Italy during the scorching summer of 1842, where Palmerston would hear nothing said against the heat that he doubtless associated with his childhood travels.

They subsequently travelled to Belgium, France, Germany and the Austrian Empire.

Events in the outside world could not, however, be ignored. In November 1841 the fecund Queen produced the awaited male heir and thus bore at least some responsibility for the verses that announced:

> A little Prince at last,
> A roaring royal boy;
> And all day long the booming bells
> Have rung their peals of joy.

In August 1842, Palmerston was able to denounce the Webster-Ashburton Treaty, which gave the United States a favourable settlement of the frontier dispute and failed to produce the mutual right of search for ships suspected of slaving, as 'a most disgraceful and disadvantageous arrangement with the Americans'. In general, he found Tory foreign policy pusillanimous and told Lord Minto in a private letter that 'the motto of the Government in foreign affairs seems to be "Give Way"'. He gave further expression to this opinion in a speech in the House of Commons on 28 July 1843 when he said: 'A wise Government in its home policy considers the reasonable wants of the people; in its foreign policy it is prepared to resist the unjust demands and the unreasonable views of foreign powers. The present Government inverts this method; it is all resistance at home, all concession abroad.'

Palmerston was a party politician and his strictures on Peel's government were not entirely fair. Despite popular enthusiasm for extreme patriotism there were dangers which ordinary voters did not appreciate sufficiently. Even with a commanding economic lead over the rest of the world, Britain could not afford to make enemies of everyone. Unless Palmerston had been prepared to advocate conscription – which would have meant political suicide – the country just did not have the resources to take on all comers. Aberdeen and Peel were probably right to see the need for a compromise settlement with the United States. Geographical considerations made it very difficult to present an effective military challenge on the west coast of America. In fact the absence of any serious military involvement in North America allowed Britain to concentrate on areas where she was likely to win any local conflict.

Certainly Palmerston was adopting an increasingly radical line in his attitude to domestic matters during these five years in opposition. His emergence as a spokesman for the working man owed a great deal to the influence of Lord Ashley (later Lord Shaftesbury). Ashley was the husband of Lady Minnie Cowper who was Lady Palmerston's daughter, and possibly Palmerston's as well; he was also a formidable campaigner for the improvement of working conditions in Britain. Palmerston supported Ashley's reforming initiatives in the Commons, including a Bill to prohibit the employment of women and young children in the mines (which was passed) and also the Ten Hours Bill which prohibited the employment of women, and of males under the age of eighteen, for more than ten hours' work per day in factories (which was not passed).

Palmerston's emergence as the champion of the oppressed may also have had something to do with the surprise visit to his London house of two trade union agents sent to lobby influential figures in Parliament. The two men got themselves invited in and then proceeded to demonstrate to Palmerston the labours required in factory work by wheeling two large chairs on castors round the dining room. Palmerston, too, pushed the chairs around, heard his wife remark 'I am glad to see your Lordship has taken yourself to work at last', and himself observed, somewhat out of breath, 'Surely this must be an exaggeration of the labour of factory workers?' But the men convinced him, and he pledged them his support.

There were other examples of Palmerston trimming his sails

to catch the radical wind. In 1842 he took up the case of a Chartist agitator who was apparently being victimised by a Black Country magistrate, and even though he made clear his disapproval for Chartist opinions, his apparently passionate concern for the freedom of speech was a marked innovation. He also spoke several times on Ireland, supporting the ideal of religious equality though insisting that the Union must be preserved, and in 1844 he held forth for three-and-a-half hours in a comprehensive denunciation of the slave-trade.

Before 1841, Palmerston had been one of the most reactionary members of the Whig government in matters of domestic affairs. Perhaps the main reason for this was that his work at the Foreign Office was so demanding that he just did not have time to give much attention to study what was going on in other departments. A period in opposition gave him an opportunity to get away from the world of diplomatic dispatches and to think of wider issues. Obviously Palmerston's increasing identification with the common man was a useful weapon in the coming struggle for power – but there was more to it than that. In many ways Palmerston was a figure from the past; he was a representative of the eighteenth century – rakish, immoral and slightly cynical. He was finding himself in a world where his own class appeared to be surrendering their values to upper middle class prudery and sentimental religiosity.

Palmerston may well have felt that the ordinary people were less contaminated by such humbug than other sections of society. Eighteenth-century aristocrats probably had closer contact with the people than their Victorian successors were to enjoy. Palmerston came from a world where aristocrats tumbled maids, fought professional prize fighters with bare fists and mingled with jockeys, ordinary punters and even criminals on the race track. Such a man knew the people and liked them for what they were. For more sensitive Victorian souls, the lower classes were interesting only in so far as they were capable of moral improvement. In some ways Palmerston was far better equipped to become the Friend of the People than later generations of politicians could be.

By 1846 his period in opposition drew to its close. The Tory prime minister Peel decided to abandon the hallowed, though recently much criticised, system of fiscal protection, and to plump for the repeal of the Corn Laws. There was great pressure from Radicals and Whigs for free trade, and when the potato crop failure of 1846 brought famine to Ireland and hunger to much of Britain it seemed essential to lay hands on cheap alternative forms of food, even if foreign produced. The Duke of Wellington put it crisply when he said, 'Rotten potatoes have done it all; they have put Peel in his d--d fright.' At any rate, having repealed the Corn Laws Peel resigned, his party torn with conflict, the Whigs were back, and so was Palmerston.

5

THE STRONG ARM
OF ENGLAND
1846-51

THE WHIG GOVERNMENT that took office in June 1846 was led
by Lord John Russell. Melbourne had become dangerously ill
in 1842 and few were able seriously to contemplate his
resuming the premiership. Palmerston considered that his
stricken brother-in-law 'had for a long time past been in the
habit of eating and drinking too much, and taking exercise too
little. Bacon says a man ought to make exercise a religion, and
be punctual in the observance of it.' Whatever the merits of this
robust diagnosis of the failing Melbourne, the elevation of the
rather prim though fairly radical Lord John Russell provided
Palmerston with a much more awkward working partner, even
though the new prime minister held his Foreign Secretary in
some awe.

When, in December 1845, Russell had made an abortive
attempt to form a government, there had been some strong
opposition to Palmerston taking the Foreign Office, on the
grounds that he would wreck Anglo-French relations. Though
in June 1846 he eventually returned to the command of foreign
affairs, there were still those who feared for the country's good
relations with France and the United States. Palmerston at first
did his best to allay these misgivings, and was particularly
accommodating to the American government over the Oregon

boundary dispute, and even over the Mexican War of 1846 – despite the Mexican government's attempt to bring Britain into the fighting by offering them the province of California!

Palmerston's diagnosis of the state of Europe in 1846 included the conviction that 'Italy is the weak part of Europe, and the next war that breaks out in Europe will probably arise out of Italian affairs . . . France and Austria would then fight each other in Italy, and France would have all the Italians on her side.' French ambitions, however, were to be expressed first in Spain.

Queen Isabella and her younger sister, Luisa, were now of marriageable age, and the choice of their bridegrooms was of crucial importance for the diplomatic equilibrium of Europe. The candidature of Louis Philippe's sons, the Duke of Aumale and the Duke of Montpensier, for the hands of the two Infantas was quite unacceptable to Britain since it threatened to rub out the Pyrenees and link France and Spain. One-and-a-half centuries before a similar threat had resulted in the protracted War of the Spanish Succession, but in 1843 Lord Aberdeen, Peel's Foreign Secretary, had managed to negotiate a compromise with the French government. Under this agreement the French withdrew their candidate, the Duke of Aumale, for Queen Isabella's hand, while keeping the Duke of Montpensier in the field for the Infanta Luisa; for their part the British government promised to drop their support for Prince Leopold of Saxe-Coburg. It was further agreed that Montpensier should not marry Luisa until Isabella was married. The task of finding a suitable husband for the Spanish Queen was not, however, easy: there were two cousins, Don Francisco, Duke of Cadiz, and Don Enrique, Duke of Seville. But Don Francisco was misshapen and impotent and thus did not commend himself to the nubile Isabella, while Don Enrique was a Radical and hence unacceptable to the French government, Metternich and the Northern powers, and Isabella's own mother.

Palmerston favoured the claims of Don Enrique, and almost immediately after returning to the Foreign Office he wrote a dispatch to Henry Bulwer, the Minister in Madrid, telling him that, in his opinion, there were now three candidates: Prince Leopold, Don Francisco and Don Enrique. He then proceeded to berate the lack of political freedom in Spain, and wrote: 'After a struggle of now thirty-four Years' duration for constitutional freedom, Spain finds herself under a system of Govt. almost as Arbitrary in practice, whatever it may be in theory, as any which ever existed in any former period of her history.'

The day after composing this hard-hitting dispatch, which could be interpreted as reneging on Aberdeen's earlier commitment to drop the candidature of Prince Leopold, Palmerston received a visit from Count Jarnac, the French chargé d'affaires in London. Palmerston was at pains to assure Jarnac of his good will, and encouraged him to take a copy of the dispatch to Bulwer to show to Louis Philippe and his Foreign Minister, Guizot. Though Palmerston has been criticised for taking the gamble of entrusting the dispatch to Jarnac, it may be said in his defence that he was understandably anxious to maintain Anglo-French accord.

The French government, however, mistrusted Palmerston's good will and bitterly remembered their humiliation in 1840 during the Near Eastern crisis of that year. Louis Philippe and Guizot proceeded to show Palmerston's dispatch to the Spanish prime minister and the Queen Mother; in the midst of their outrage, the French government proposed that Isabella should at once marry Don Francisco, and the Duke of Montpensier the Infanta Luisa – thus giving France the match that would bear progeny and provide a great diplomatic triumph.

While these plans were being hatched, Palmerston was accompanying the Queen and Prince Albert on a Channel cruise aboard the *Victoria and Albert* in the first week of September. It

81

was a curious affair, providing ample illustration of Albert's serious cast of mind, for the indefatigable prince compared Jersey to the Bay of Naples, spent innumerable hours in collecting geological specimens, sketched St Michael's Mount and held forth on a wide variety of topics. At Fowey he led the men down to a mine, where 'Albert and the gentlemen wore miners' hats'. Lady Palmerston had already resignedly remarked of Albert that 'Whatever he does amuses him', but Victoria was enthralled by his activities, though on one occasion Palmerston induced her to stay on board while the Prince hunted down more rocky specimens. The royal couple were accompanied by their first-born son, the five-year-old Prince Albert Edward, dressed in a sailor suit; at Penryn the Mayor and Corporation came out to pay their respects, and Queen Victoria recorded contentedly: 'I stepped out of the pavilion on deck with Bertie, and Lord Palmerston told them that that was "The Duke of Cornwall".'

But at Penzance these harmless trivialities were rudely interrupted by the staggering news of the French coup over the Spanish marriages. Palmerston's formal protest to the Spanish government was icily rebuffed; Guizot defended himself by arguing that Palmerston had worked secretly to promote the marital fortunes of Leopold of Saxe-Coburg; Metternich refused to become involved. On 10 October the double marriages took place; the unfortunate Isabella, however, was soon able to console herself with lovers, thus moving Prince Albert to the pious sentiment that 'The Queen has her lovers. What will Louis Philippe have to answer for in heaven!'

Palmerston, though incensed, like most of British opinion from Queen Victoria downwards, over the Spanish marriages, was able to put the matter in perspective. There was, of course, no more high-flown talk of the Anglo-French 'understanding', but otherwise Palmerston tried to carry on business as usual with France. The Queen, who had been an eye-witness to the diplomatic revelation at Penzance, wrote that she 'must do Palmerston the credit to say that he takes it very quietly, and will act very temperately about it'. Palmerston took a rueful view of the whole affair and admitted that 'we have been defeated by our own timidity, hesitation, and delay. . . . Louis Philippe and Guizot, like practical and sagacious men, determined to knock us down at once, and make an apology afterwards if necessary to pacify us.' In fact, Louis Philippe's triumph did not result in the union of the French and Spanish crowns, for in February 1848 the Orleans monarchy fell and the 'Citizen King' crossed the Channel to die in Surrey two years later; and even though France was once more to accept a monarch it was the shrewd head of a Bonaparte that received the crown in 1852, not a son of Louis Philippe.

As Palmerston was struggling to adjust to the French coup in Spain, Portugal erupted into civil war. The Radical Septembrists, denied the fruits of their sweeping victory in the general election of 1845 by Queen Maria da Gloria's decision to dissolve the Cortes and annul the constitution, seized Oporto in October 1846 and established a revolutionary Junta. The Queen of Portugal appealed for help to the other members of the Quadruple Alliance (Britain, France and Spain). Palmerston was reluctant to involve Britain in active participation in the civil war, but sent the fleet to the Tagus with orders to save the Queen's life if necessary, though otherwise to remain neutral. The governments of France and Spain were, however, more anxious to intervene on behalf of Maria da Gloria. Palmerston strove to commend a compromise to both sides in Portugal, whereby the Junta would return to their allegiance to the Queen in return for the restoration of constitutional government, freedom of the press and trial by jury. When by May 1847 these proposals had not been fully accepted by the Junta, Palmerston, in agreement with France and Spain, decided on physical intervention. The Royal Navy blockaded Oporto and joint

British and Spanish forces marched against the Junta. Eventually the Septembrists surrendered and Maria da Gloria restored the constitution though maintaining the right-wing government of Marshal Saldanha in power.

Oddly, Palmerston was able to calm down the criticism of British Radicals that he had crushed the forces of liberty in Portugal by arguing that the Septembrists would have suffered a much rougher fate if Spain alone had intervened in the civil war. There was doubtless a good deal of truth in this, but the plain fact was that Marshal Saldanha remained in office. There were other complaints over Palmerston's handling of the situation: Queen Victoria, Prince Albert, Guizot, the Spanish government and those of the Northern powers were annoyed at the way in which he had forced Maria da Gloria to pardon the rebels and grant them concessions.

Victoria, prompted by Albert, voiced other complaints. In particular, that Palmerston sent off dispatches without first submitting them for royal approval. She had requested 'through Lord John Russell and personally to see that the drafts to our Foreign Ministers are not despatched *previous* to their being submitted to the Queen. Notwithstanding, this is still done, as for instance to-day with regard to the drafts for Lisbon.' There is no doubt that Palmerston from time to time deliberately gave the Queen and Albert no opportunity to alter dispatches. He apologised handsomely over the Portuguese drafts, and blamed the Foreign Office staff for failing to supply Victoria with the dispatches in question. But he was to lapse again on a good many occasions, and in 1848 the outraged royal couple demanded that Russell remove Palmerston from the Foreign Office; it was a demand that Russell was unable to fulfill, but it provided a clear indication of the stormy course that Palmerston's relationship was to run with Victoria and Albert.

While the affairs of Iberia were exercising Palmerston's talents, Ireland remained gripped by famine. The year 1847 saw the worst horrors of the 'great hunger', and by the end of the year almost 300,000 had died and many hundreds of thousands had emigrated to the United States and Canada. Although the 'hungry forties' confirmed Palmerston's belief in the benefits of free trade, he was not transformed into an open-handed benefactor of the poor and destitute. He backed the government's refusal to give any assistance to able-bodied Irishmen, even though there was no system of poor relief in Ireland.

He was also involved in a scandal over the treatment of some 2,000 tenants from his Sligo estates who emigrated to North America. Palmerston contributed to the fares of these unfortunates, and paid for hot rum punch to sustain them on their voyage (though this was subsequently changed to coffee and biscuits after representations from the priesthood and temperance societies). But Palmerston had also announced that each family would receive between £5 and £2 on arrival in Canada. Unfortunately there were no agents to meet the emigrants as they disembarked, and therefore no money was paid out. Quite apart from the fact that appalling overcrowding on the nine ships that sailed from Ireland resulted in many deaths, a large number of the bewildered men, women and children who were dumped unceremoniously in the snow-filled streets of Quebec and St John had hardly any clothing, and one woman was actually carried ashore naked and wrapped in a blanket. Protests poured in, the Canadian press fulminated, and a Canadian politician compared the conditions under which Palmerston's tenants had travelled to the horrors of the slave trade. Palmerston tried to discover the causes of this mismanagement, but his explanations had a hollow ring.

Nearer home Palmerston had to defend his seat at Tiverton during the general election of 1847. Lord John Russell went to the country hoping to gain a majority in the Commons, in which his government only continued to survive because of the split between Peelite free-trade Tories and the protectionist Tories led by Disraeli. As it happened, the election still left the Whigs five seats short of their opponents' total, but given the implacable hostility of the feuding Tory factions, Russell was able to carry on as prime minister for a further five years.

The campaign at Tiverton was made particularly lively by the candidature of a leading Chartist, Julian Harney, ably supported by Palmerston's traditional opponent, the Radical butcher Rowcliffe. The brass band thumped and blared, and an intent crowd jostled and shouted at the hustings. Harney invoked Palmerston's diabolical Tory origins, and berated him over a huge canvas of past events that ran from the infamous Six Acts and Peterloo to his recent support for Queen of Portugal against her home-grown Radicals. Then Palmerston replied, smiling, his arms folded, his ears apparently shut to the shouts of 'Ah, Cupid! Sly Cupid!' He spoke for three hours, and the reporters from the leading London newspapers present took it down word for word. Casting aside the somewhat pompous and evasive style he habitually employed at the dispatch box, Palmerston treated his audience to a good-humoured, forceful and direct defence of his policies – spiced with a few oratorical sleights of hand. Typical of his robust delivery was his account of the Opium War: 'We said to the Chinese, "You have behaved very ill; we have had to teach you better manners; it has cost us something to do it, but we will send our bill in, and you must pay our charges." That was done, and they have certainly profited by the lesson. They have become free traders too.'

Despite his hearty exposition of British foreign policy, when Palmerston finished he was soundly defeated on a show of hands – mostly Chartists' hands. He then demanded a proper poll; Harney withdrew in protest against an electoral system which still disenfranchised the vast majority of adults, and Palmerston and his colleague Heathcote were returned unopposed.

As 1847 drew to a close, Palmerston was busy with Channel defences which he considered open to surprise attacks under the cover of fog, with the heightening tension in Italy where Metternich was pouring Austrian reinforcements into Lombardy, and with some recent outrages against Protestants in Ireland which prompted him to the sobering reflection that 'the true remedy cannot in these days be applied, but if you *could* hang the Priests of the Parish whenever a murder such as these last was committed, I have a notion that Protestant life would be much more secure'.

He was also deeply involved in the brief Swiss Civil War where, in November 1847, and allegedly at his instigation, the Liberal Federal government forcibly asserted its authority over the secessionist Sonderbund - a league of seven predominantly Catholic cantons. Austria, Prussia, France and, finally, Russia were prepared to move against the triumphant Swiss Liberals. If this had occurred, there would have been little that Palmerston could have done to save them. As it happened, the 1848 revolutions throughout Europe saved Swiss Liberalism.

The year of revolutions, 1848, opened with uprisings in Sicily in January; soon the tremors had spread to other parts of Italy. In February, the people of Paris rose in revolt; a month later Vienna and Berlin witnessed popular uprisings directed against autocratic government and unconstitutional practices. Soon all of Europe from the Channel to the borders of Russia was in a ferment of revolution and counter-revolution. Kings, princes and ministers fled before the storm, 'running about', in Thomas Carlyle's description, 'like a gang of coiners when the police come among them'. Soon many of these notables were washed up on the benevolent shores of Britain, 'the King of France in a Surrey villa, Metternich in a Hanover Square Hotel, and the Prince of Prussia at Lady Palmerston's'; Guizot, too, reached London.

For his part, Palmerston, though no lover of revolutions,

must have taken some pleasure at the sight of most of his greatest adversaries huddled in exile in Britain while he still held sway at the Foreign Office. He indeed noted with relish 'the sweep made of the Plotters of the Spanish Marriages; and what is most poetical in the Retribution is that they have all of them been themselves the active agents of their own Destruction'.

Still, even though Palmerston could, on the one hand, gloat over the destruction of Guizot's plans to construct an anti-British alliance, and, on the other, recoil from communist revolutionary manifestations (telling the British Minister in Munich in April 1848 that 'The Struggle now going on in many parts of Europe is one between those who have no property and those who have and wish to keep it') he made plain his determination to pursue British interests throughout. Palmerston gave clear expression to his policy in a lengthy speech in the House of Commons on 1 March, filling fifty-seven columns of Hansard in the process. In the course of his speech he declared: 'I hold with respect to alliances that England is a Power sufficiently strong, sufficiently powerful to steer her own course, and not to tie herself as an unnecessary appendage to the policy of any other Government. I hold that the real policy of England - apart from questions which involve her own particular interests, political or commercial - is to be the champion of justice and right, pursuing that course with moderation and prudence, not becoming the Quixote of the world, but giving the weight of her moral sanction and support wherever she thinks that justice is, and wherever she thinks that wrong has been done. . . . It is a narrow policy to suppose that this country or that is to be marked out as the eternal ally or the perpetual enemy of England. We have no eternal allies, we have no perpetual enemies. Our interests are eternal and perpetual, and those interests it is our duty to follow.'

At the same time, Palmerston had considerable sympathy for

The young Viscount Palmerston in the year of his father's death, 1802,
when he was seventeen. A water-colour by T. Heaphy.

ABOVE Broadlands, near Romsey in Hampshire, was the birthplace and country seat of Lord Palmerston. His father, the second Viscount, spent £23,000 on its improvement and employed Capability Brown to landscape the grounds.

LEFT Lord Palmerston drawn by Geoffrey Richmond

Emily Lamb, Lady Palmerston, painted by John Lucas in 1840. She was the sister of William Lamb, Lord Melbourne and married first Lord Cowper and then Lord Palmerston.

CUPID OUT OF PLACE.

A *Punch* cartoon of 1841 depicting Palmerston as 'Lord Cupid', a nickname he earned through his numerous alleged love affairs.

A *Punch* cartoon on Palmerston's dismissal from the Foreign Office in 1851. Victoria was delighted at his fall from power but Palmerston was so enraged that he ignored an appointment with the Queen to hand over the seals of office.

THERE'S ALWAYS SOMETHING.

A *Punch* cartoon published 31 December 1853 on Palmerston's temporary resignation. It shows that although it was formally over a proposal to extend the franchise, differences of policy over war with Russia were believed to be behind it. Austria is represented by the two-headed Habsburg eagle.

THE MINISTERIAL SPLIT.

The Aberdeen Cabinet meets to decide on the Crimean expedition in February 1854. Standing, left to right: Sir Charles Wood, Sir William Molesworth, the Duke of Argyll, the Earl of Clarendon, the Duke of Newcastle. Seated, left to right: William Gladstone, Marquis Lansdowne, Lord John Russell, Earl Granville, the Earl of Aberdeen, Lord Cranworth, Viscount Palmerston, Sir George Grey, Sidney Herbert and the Duke of Newcastle.

NOW FOR IT!

A Set-to between "Pam, the Downing Street Pet," and "The Russian Spider."

A *Punch* cartoon of 1855 illustrating the confidence felt in Palmerston's ability to handle the Crimean War.

Palmerston's popularity with the general public is shown by this grand reception held at Romsey in 1855 on his arrival for a visit to Broadlands.

BELOW A *Punch* cartoon on Palmerston's determination to hold out for harsh peace terms in the Crimean War. In fact the French unwillingness to continue the war forced him to compromise.

MINIÉ CARTRIDGES

CRIMEA

RUSSIA.   AUSTRIA.   PALMERSTON.

WHAT IS THE PRICE OF PEACE?

Palmerston in the House of Commons, 1860. Seated behind him left to right
are Lord John Russell, Gladstone, Sir George Grey, Sir Charles Wood and
Sir George Cornwall Lewis (holding notebook). Opposite sits Disraeli with
Lord Stanley, Major-General Peel and Sir Edward Lytton Bulwer Lytton to
his right. Richard Cobden and John Bright are standing below the balcony
on the left.

BELOW Palmerston's study at Broadlands with the high desk at which he
worked.

Lord and Lady Palmerston in old age. They still held zestful and lavish parties in London and at Broadlands, entertaining guests with tales of their youthful scandals.

BELOW The funeral procession of Lord Palmerston reaches the door of Westminster Abbey, 4 November 1865.

European nationalist sentiment (even though he was less than sympathetic towards, say, Chinese or Afghan nationalism). He gave expression to these feelings, and simultaneously aimed an indirect blow at Metternich, when he argued:

Providence meant mankind to be divided into separate nations, and for this purpose countries have been bounded by natural barriers, and races of men have been distinguished by separate languages, habits, manners, dispositions, and characters. There is no case on the globe where this intention is more marked than that of the Italians and the Germans, kept apart by the Alps, and as unlike in every thing as two races can be. Austria has never possessed Italy as part of her Empire, but has always held it as a conquered territory. There has been no mixture of races. The only Austrians have been the troops and the civil officers. She has governed it as you govern a garrison town, and her rule has always been hateful.

His reactions to the tumultuous events of 1848-9 were, understandably, as varied as the British interests involved, yet, though he was able to write 'Vive Lamartine' with some conviction, he remained wary of radical excess and regretted that 'the example of universal franchise in France will set our non-voting population agog, and will create a demand for an inconvenient extension of the suffrage, ballot, and other mischevious things'. He also disliked republics, thought that 'Large republics seem to be essentially and inherently aggressive', and feared that republican France would consequently cause war in Europe. Despite these prejudices, he adjusted well enough to the new diplomatic pieces on the European chessboard, and accepted Lamartine and other leaders thrown up by the revolution as phlegmatically as he had previously dealt with Guizot and Metternich.

Palmerston was a warm supporter of the revolution in Spain, and a less warm supporter of the revolutionary movements in France and Italy. In the case of Hungary he wished the Austrians had been better able to keep their own house in order, though he later took up the British public's protests at General

Haynau's atrocities against the Hungarians. In essence, of course, he had little real chance to influence events: his dispatches could not turn Windischgrätz away from Prague, or halt the Russian march on Hungary, or prevent the firing squads of King 'Bomba' from thinning the ranks of Neapolitan Radicals. Indeed, whether or not Palmerston supported them, the revolutionaries were, by the end of 1849, swept off the board in Germany, the Austrian Empire, Italy and Spain, while the French settled for Louis Napoleon, nephew of the great Bonaparte, as the Prince-President of the Second Republic. Only in the duchy of Schleswig-Holstein, balanced uneasily between the twin pulls of Prussia and Denmark, could Palmerston claim a major success, and the duchy continued as before to be linked to Denmark through the rule of the Danish King as Grand Duke.

In Britain the revolutionary convulsions that raged throughout Europe found their expression in the great Chartist demonstration of 10 April 1848. The Chartists assembled on Kennington Green and announced their intention of marching on the House of Commons. The demonstration was officially banned, the troops called out under the Duke of Wellington, and 175,000 special constables were enrolled. Palmerston was in charge of the special constables whose job was to defend the Foreign Office; Lady Palmerston with her daughter Lady Ashley, strolled down to see him and was impressed by the good-fellowship and spirit of equality shown by the special constables – who were drawn from the gentry, the middle classes and loyal working men. The great demonstration reached Westminster Bridge, but dispersed when they realised they were faced with troops. Though the English revolution never materialised, there was more serious disorder in famine-stricken Ireland, though Palmerston thought little would come of it since 'men must eat to be able to fight'.

Despite his lack of success in supporting certain revolutionary movements in Europe between 1848-9, Palmerston remained a hero to Radicals on both sides of the Channel. Not only that, his steadfast protection of British interests and British subjects abroad gave him a special place in the affections of all sections of the British public. Though some members of the aristocracy and the Nonconformist middle class deplored his bullying methods, the majority of Britons were doubtless proud that the long arm of Palmerston and the Royal Navy could protect them throughout the globe.

Nothing better illustrates the appeal of Palmerston's gunboat diplomacy than the Don Pacifico affair of 1850. The grievances of Don (or Mr) Pacifico against the Greek government did not stand in isolation; in 1836 a Scottish historian, George Finlay, living in Athens, had his garden taken to provide a site for a royal palace and did not receive a drachma in compensation until a meagre offer was made in 1847; there was also friction over British rule in the Ionian Islands which had begun in 1815 and reached the depths of unpopularity by 1848. Don Pacifico was a Portuguese Jew who had been born in Gibraltar and was therefore a British subject. During Easter 1847, a predictable outburst of anti-semitic agitation resulted in an Athenian mob breaking into his house, where they manhandled his family, stole some valuables and then set fire to the property.

Pacifico claimed £5,000 in damages from the Greek government and an additional £27,000 for some documents, allegedly destroyed in the fire, which proved his claim to that much compensation from the Portuguese government. The Greek government expressed its regret for Pacifico's misfortunes but insisted that it could not be held responsible for the actions of the mob. Pacifico then directed a special plea to Palmerston claiming that 'a strong hand, a firm will, are necessary to compel the Greek Government to perform a duty of equity and of justice. That strong hand can only be yours, my Lord; that firm will my just rights lead me to hope will be yours likewise.'

It is probable, however, that Palmerston would not have sent the Royal Navy to terrorise the Greek government if it had not already conveniently been in the Eastern Mediterranean to support the Turkish government in a wrangle with Austria and Russia over the presence of Hungarian and Polish refugees (including Kossuth and Bern) in Turkish territory. As it was, Palmerston ordered the fleet to Athens at the end of 1849; it arrived off Piraeus, the port of Athens, on 15 January 1850. Wyse, the British Minister in Greece, then presented an ultimatum to the Greek government demanding payment of £31,000 to Pacifico, with interest at 12 per cent since 1847, and £750 for Finlay, with interest at 12 per cent since 1836, within twenty-four hours; if the government refused the Royal Navy would act against Greek shipping.

While the Greek ministers made a bid for more time, the twenty-four hours expired and Admiral Parker proceeded to seize Greek ships and to blockade Piraeus and other Greek ports. Many Greek opponents of King Otho's regime actually seem to have welcomed the British action, but foreign governments were incensed, as were the Queen and the Tory party at home. Formal protests flowed into London, and the French ambassador was withdrawn. Eventually Don Pacifico received £6,400 for damages caused by the fire and, a year later, a paltry (but not inappropriate) £150 for his missing documents. Palmerston's intervention, therefore, had only partly achieved its object.

In June 1850 Palmerston rose in the Commons to defend his foreign policy against vehement criticism. His speech provided him with the greatest Parliamentary triumph of his career. He made an appeal to national pride, chauvinism even, and also to Radical dislike of King Otho of Greece. His speech contained a review of his policy from 1830, from 'the sunny plains of Castile and the gay vineyards of France ... to the mountains of Switzerland'. Then he unleashed a peroration that he had learned by heart, and struck a resounding chord among the early Victorian public:

I do not complain of the conduct of those who have made these matters the means of attack upon Her Majesty's Ministers. The Government of a great country like this, is undoubtedly an object of fair and legitimate ambition to men of all shades of opinion. It is a noble thing to be allowed to guide the policy and to influence the destinies of such a country; and, if ever it was an object of honourable ambition, more than ever it be so at the moment at which I am speaking. For while we have seen, as stated by the Right Honourable Baronet the Member for Ripon, the political earthquake rocking Europe from side to side - while we have seen thrones shaken, shattered, levelled; institutions overthrown and destroyed - while in almost every country of Europe the conflict of civil war has deluged the land with blood from the Atlantic to the Black Sea, from the Baltic to the Mediterranean; this country has represented a spectacle honourable to the people of England, and worthy of the admiration of mankind.

We have shown that liberty is compatible with order; that individual freedom is reconcilable with obedience to the law. We have shown the example of a nation, in which every class of society accepts with cheerfulness the lot which Providence has assigned to it; while at the same time every individual of each class is constantly striving to raise himself in the social scale - not by injustice and wrong, not by violence and illegality - but by persevering good conduct, and by the steady and energetic exertion of the moral and intellectual faculties with which his Creator has endowed him. To govern such a people as this is indeed an object worthy of the ambition of the noblest man who lives in the land; and, therefore, I find no fault with those who may think any opportunity a fair one, for endeavouring to place themselves in so distinguished and honourable a position. But I contend that we have not in our foreign policy done anything to forfeit the confidence of the country. . . . I therefore fearlessly challenge the verdict which this House, as representing a political, a commercial, a constitutional country, is to give on the question now brought before it; whether the principles on which the foreign policy of Her Majesty's Government has been conducted, and the sense of duty which has led us to think ourselves bound to afford protection to our fellow subjects abroad, are proper and fitting guides for those who are charged with the government of England; and whether, as the Roman, in days of old, held himself free from indignity, when he could say Civis Romanus sum; so also a British subject, in whatever land he may be, shall feel confident that the watchful eye and the strong arm of England will protect him against injustice and wrong.

When he sat down the cheers rolled round him unceasingly; he had spoken for four hours and thirty-five minutes, but to Lady Palmerston, whose eyes never left his face, it seemed to last merely an hour. The opposition to Palmerston was drowned in the acclaim that poured in from the benches of the Commons and, later, from the public in the constituencies. The speech was a tremendous success: Palmerston's political opponents could not, for the moment, stand up to him. Throughout the country he was acclaimed by an astounding variety of people: the middle class and working men; backwoods squires and Radicals; Manchester businessmen and country solicitors. Palmerston revelled in his triumph, and the government received a majority of forty-six at the end of the debate.

Why did the Don Pacifico speech strike such a resounding chord with the British public? Part of the answer lies in the feeling of security which Palmerston's words gave to his fellow-subjects; it really did seem to ordinary Britons that their interests would be protected on a world-wide scale. As the Radical Roebuck claimed, the Tsar could send any of his subjects to Siberia at a moment's notice, but Palmerston would never let him do the same to a British subject. Another Radical, Bernard Osborne, proclaimed of Palmerston: 'This proved his worth; hereafter be our boast: Who hated Britons hated him the most.'

Palmerston had also, once again, caught the spirit of the age. Early-Victorian Britain was not ashamed to flex its muscles and to exert its influence. Palmerston was saying, like a triumphant, tousled schoolboy faced with a variety of opponents, 'here I stand. Knock me down if you can! Knock me down if you dare!'

In fact, in congratulating Palmerston for his pugnacity, the British people were congratulating themselves. It was a sure formula for public acclaim.

Palmerston's remarkable popularity did him surprisingly little good at Buckingham Palace. Victoria, supported by her Prince (whose imagination was already feasting on the glories of a Great Exhibition of Britain's scientific and technological achievements), wanted him out of the Foreign Office. The royal couple had a long catalogue of complaints that included the unseemly scuffle with the virtuous lady-in-waiting at Windsor, Palmerston's apparent enthusiasm for the overthrow of European crowned heads, and, of course, his endless capacity for altering (or simply not showing) dispatches. Lord John Russell tried to mediate; Palmerston made shows of repentance (once, so Albert noted, with tears in his eyes); but matters did not mend.

Another cause of friction arose when the notorious Austrian General Haynau, who had been responsible for a number of atrocities during the crushing of the 1848 revolutions in Italy and Hungary, visited Britain in September 1850. When the general (known as 'General Hyena' to the British public) visited Barclay's brewery at Southwark he was set about by the workers and thrashed. The Queen was appalled at this episode, but Palmerston sent an unrepentant dispatch to Vienna, and privately informed the Home Secretary that the mob should have 'tossed him in a blanket, rolled him in the kennel, and sent him home in a cab, paying his fare to the hotel'. Under renewed royal pressure, Palmerston in fact sent a second, more accommodating, dispatch to Austria.

But Palmerston's time as Foreign Secretary was drawing to a stormy close. In December 1851 he voiced his approval of Louis Napoleon's recent coup d'état, in which the President had dissolved the National Assembly and arrested prominent Republicans, to the French ambassador in London, Count

Walewski. But his dispatches to Paris commended neutrality as the British attitude to the coup; a hiatus followed; the Queen once more complained about dispatches being sent off before she could alter them, and demanded Palmerston's dismissal. John Russell knew that Palmerston would have no Radical backing over the Walewski indiscretion, and wrote him a curt note dismissing him from office and offering him (almost insultingly) the Lord Lieutenantship of Ireland and (less insultingly) a peerage of the United Kingdom. Palmerston was furious at his dismissal; he failed to deliver up his seals of office at Windsor on 26 December 1851, and Russell had to do it for him. Radical opinion denounced his overthrow; so did a number of newspapers, as well as countless foursquare Englishmen.

An outraged Lady Palmerston wrote on 8 January 1852:

> *Broadlands,*
> *Wednesday.*

My Dearest Fred,

I believe I forgot to tell you in my letter yesterday that John had offered to Palmerston to go Ld. Lieut. to Ireland with a Peerage which he refused at once – it was in the letter which I mentioned yes[y] among the facts of the case – John has behaved shamefully ill to Pal[n], and I suppose there never was such a case before of a man throwing over a Colleague & a Friend without the slightest reason to give for it.

No doubt the Queen & Prince wanted to get Palmerston out & Granville in because they thought he would be pliable & subservient and would let Albert manage the Foreign Office which is what he had always wanted – you may think it lucky therefore that the dream of United Germany & the Sleswick-Holstein business are now pretty nearly over.

John has behaved like a little Blackguard giving in to their plans and trying to put it upon a private opinion expressed to Valesky (which bound the Governm[t] to no course, and left it quite unshackled).

The Times article today is full of false statements, for there are no differences now between Pal[n] & any Governments or any foreign ministers, nor are there any differences at home.

We have often seen that many of his Colleagues were jealous of him, but apparently they were all on the best possible terms and there were no points in dispute.

I think the House of Commons will be very angry at this Granville appointment – a young Lordling who has done nothing but dance attendance on Albert & patch up differences amongst the Crystal Palace Commissioners, who has whispered a speech or two about the Board of Trade & the one at Paris in which he put forward his having passed his holidays in his Father's Home at Paris & having married a French woman.

He has a good deal of tact & is very courteous & those are his real merits & that is what makes him so Popular.

I am still vexed & provoked at the whole thing but I take it much more calmly. It is so lucky for an effervescing Woman to have such a calm and placid husband which no events can irritate, or make him lose his temper.

* * * * * * *

We have had a lovely day & very bright but cold, Georgᵃ without her hat sitting under our great magnolia.

The best thing that can happen in my opinion would be the break-up of this Governmᵗ and to let the Protectionists have a try. We should then see whether the land could be relieved, whether there can be any duty on corn, and what changes can be made – and I think it would be fair enough to see that side of the question tried. . . .

But it was the Chartist newspaper *Reynold's Weekly*, that spoke for the masses when it proclaimed:

> Small John has been and gone
> And turned adrift Lord Palmerston,
> Amongst the lot the only don,
> Who didn't take care of number one;
> Out spoke Home Secretary Gray,
> I wish old Palmy was away.
> Aye, turn him out they all did say,
> For he's the people's darling.

6
HOME SECRETARY
1852-5

PALMERSTON at first accepted his dismissal from the Foreign Office, if not with good grace, at least passively. He thought of commissioning a scurrilous pamphlet attacking Albert, the foreign meddler, but then dropped the idea before the pamphlet could be circulated. When in February 1852 Parliament reassembled, his Radical supporters in the Commons brought up the question of his dismissal. Lord John Russell, however, cut the ground from under Palmerston's feet once more by revealing the facts concerning his support for Louis Napoleon's coup d'état and his sending of dispatches without submitting them to the Queen. Russell also revealed the text of an angry memorandum from Victoria, on the perennial subject of dispatches, to which Palmerston had meekly submitted in order to stay in office.

Palmerston now had to choose between denouncing the royal view of ministerial responsibility and conduct, which he had previously accepted, or to lie low. Although he protested in private that 'I had no reason to suppose that this memorandum would ever be seen by, or known to, anybody but the Queen, John Russell and myself', he prudently decided not to risk a violent collision with the monarchy – thus sacrificing some Radical support.

There was every reason to suppose, however, that even if he dodged the constitutional point, he would make a spirited defence of his policy, after the fashion of his Don Pacifico speech. The street ballad singers expected him to rout his enemies as before:

> Whene'er doth meet the Parliament,
> The Whigs to pot will straight be sent,
> That humbug of a Government
>> Won't live a moment longer.
> Then Palmy he'll be at our head,
> And keep the tyrants all in dread,
> Austria and France will wish him dead
> And for milksop in his stead,
> Haynau and the Russian Tsar
> Will curse him in their realms afar.
> And on their feeling it will jar
>> To find old Palmy stronger.

Palmerston did indeed rise to speak in his own defence in the Commons in February, but it was overall a poor, mangled performance, and Disraeli straightway compared him to a 'beaten fox'. He did, however, conjure up a flash of his old fire with the wry observation that 'every member of the Cabinet . . . is at liberty to express an opinion on passing events abroad; but the Secretary of State for Foreign Affairs, whose peculiar duty is to watch over those events and to form an opinion – who is unfit for his office if he has not an opinion on them – is the only man not permitted to express any opinion at all; and when a Foreign Minister comes and tells him news, he is to remain speechless, like a gaping dolt, or as silent as the mute of some Eastern Pasha.' But this oratorical flourish did not satisfy the House, and even when Palmerston made a bid for renewed Radical support with some words on slavery the effect was disappointing.

In the London clubs the verdict was that 'Palmerston is smashed', and Disraeli rashly claimed that 'there *was* a Palmerston'. Palmerston was, however, more resilient than that. He made some use of his enforced leisure at Broadlands, where he shot in the mornings and inspected his estate; he found the garden neglected, for 'it is a trial to a man to be left as much alone and unlooked after as the gardener of a Secretary of State necessarily is', and sacked the gardener.

But in reality Palmerston, though no longer Foreign Secretary, had several options open to him. The state of the parties in the House of Commons early in 1852 made various political combinations possible since there were 330 Whigs (including the Radicals), some 200 Tories, led by the Earl of Derby, about 100 Peelites (led by Lord Aberdeen following Peel's death in 1850) and 35 Irish Nationalists. Popular enthusiasm for Palmerston was still so great that whatever Queen Victoria and Russell may have wished, the former Foreign Secretary was an important force in politics. In conditions of political chaos, without a rigid, two party system, personalities were bound to count for more than they had done in the 1830s. Russell's government had not been an outstanding success. Despite the prime minister's undoubted abilities, he was a man who took up an enthusiasm to the virtual exclusion of all else, whether or not there was any political mileage to be made from the cause. 'Little Johnny' was liable to make himself ridiculous and just did not have the same charismatic appeal as Palmerston. Should Palmerston try to oust Russell from the leadership of the Whig party, should he join the Derby Tories, should he make some arrangement with the Peelites or should he work towards a completely new political alignment? For a moment it looked as if he would choose the Tories.

Seventeen days after Palmerston's defence of his conduct over the Walewski affair had flopped so badly, he was instrumental in turning John Russell's government out. On 20

February Palmerston's amendment to the government Militia Bill was carried by thirteen votes, and Russell promptly resigned, causing the fallen Foreign Secretary to 'conclude that the Cabinet were glad to make use of the Militia Question as a convenient Parachute to avoid a ruder Descent and a more dangerous one'. Lord Derby was invited to form a government, but the Tories (or Conservatives as they now preferred to be called) were a minority party in the Commons; Derby needed any powerful allies he could persuade to join his administration. The obvious man to approach was Palmerston, who was now sloughing off his Radical guise, was at odds with Russell and the Whigs, and had earlier been a staunch Tory. Disraeli, indeed, had already told Derby that 'it is everything for your Government that P. should be a member of it. His prestige in the House is very great; in the country considerable. He will not give you trouble about principles, but he may about *position*. He would not like to serve under me.'

In fact, Palmerston did give trouble over one principle. As a convinced free trader, with the traces of his old Edinburgh professor's fiscal certainties still coursing through his veins, he would not join the Conservatives while they still clung to protection. He therefore refused Derby's offer of the now prestigious post of Chancellor of the Exchequer, and Disraeli took over at the Treasury instead. He was favourably inclined to Derby's government in some respects, however, even if he confessed that 'having acted for twenty-two years with the Whigs, and after having gained by, and while acting with them, any little political reputation I may have acquired it would not . . . be at all agreeable to me to go slap over the opposite camp, and this merely on account of a freak of John Russell's, which the whole Whig party regretted and condemned'.

One way in which Palmerston showed his good will towards Derby's government was to give a helping hand to the new Foreign Secretary Lord Malmesbury, the grandson of his old guardian and mentor. He gave Malmesbury a thorough survey of foreign affairs and urged him to keep in well with France, explaining that Britain and France were rivals in the Near East 'like two men in love with the same woman'. He also told his youthful successor that 'he could have no idea . . . what a power of *prestige* England possesses abroad', and urged him not to lose it. Palmerston also had some advice on departmental business and sang the praises of plain handwriting with appropriate spaces between the lines.

But these labours, and a visit to his Sligo estates (where his tenants announced their devotion to 'the British Empire and yer honour's family, and it's proud we are to see ye in the Far West'), were not especially exhausting. He attended the Commons regularly, however, concerning himself (as usual) with national defence, and spoke in favour of preserving the Crystal Palace – a timely sop to royal sensibilities in the aftermath of the Great Exhibition.

More exhilarating was the general election of July 1852. Palmerston went down to Tiverton to do ritual battle with the doughty Rowcliffe. But though he lodged himself as usual at the 'Three Tuns', and occupied the same four-poster bed as on previous occasions, the tone of his hustings speech was different. Though he continued to criticise the Chartists, he went out of his way to avoid offending the Conservatives and did not belabour the free-trade controversy. Rowcliffe, sensing that he was angling for Conservative support, asked him point-blank what government he meant to join. Palmerston replied, 'Now that is a question that must depend upon the future; but I will tell him what Government I do not mean to join. I can assure you and him that I will never join a Government called a Rowcliffe Administration'.

Elsewhere in his speech Palmerston praised the virtues of British tradition, spoke in favour of increased expenditure on national defence, and poured scorn on the idea of voting by secret ballot, since 'a true Englishman hates doing a thing in secret or in the dark' and would deplore 'sneaking to the ballot-box and poking in a piece of paper, looking round to see that no one could read it'. In short, Lady Palmerston was more than justified in her opinion that she had never seen 'anything better, so clever, so witty, so exactly all one could wish and *dans le fond* so conservative'.

When the election results were declared, Palmerston was returned for Tiverton, and the Conservatives gained more than 100 seats from their Whig and Peelite opponents. Though lacking an overall majority, the Conservatives had 310 seats, the Whigs 270, the Peelites 40 and the Irish Nationalists 40. Realising, nonetheless, that fiscal protection was a liability in the constituencies, the Conservatives now declared themselves in favour of free trade; the Whigs put down a vote of censure accusing their opponents of political opportunism, and Palmerston stepped in to move an amendment welcoming the Conservative's change of heart. The amendment was carried, and Palmerston had demonstrated his willingness to save Lord Derby's government.

In December 1852, however, the government were defeated in a vote on Disraeli's supplementary budget. Derby resigned, and Lord Aberdeen (Palmerston's contemporary at Harrow) became prime minister, with a cabinet nicely balanced between Peelites and Whigs. The alliance of Whigs and Peelites helped to justify Palmerston's own defection from the Tory party. A new wave of Tory renegades were following the path to the Left he had taken twenty years earlier. Palmerston always put administrative competence high on the list of his priorities and the Peelites would provide a welcome boost of talent and experience. But, in a curious way, Palmerston's attitude now was not unlike that of the Russells and Hollands in the early 1830s; he felt that the Peelites were given more jobs in the new administration than their numbers justified. In fact, Palmerston disliked the Peelites intensely. They were indentified with the kind of 'appeasement' foreign policy he abhorred and they almost wallowed in respectability and religious fervour. Pious young men like William Ewart Gladstone had little in common with Palmerston, except a capacity for hard work. The eighteenth and nineteenth centuries stared each other in the face and neither cared for what they saw.

Of course Palmerston was a front-runner for high office, his cause discreetly urged on by Lady Palmerston, who was beginning to feel the pinch of his loss of departmental salary. But there were difficulties: the Queen and Prince Albert were determined never again to have him as Foreign Secretary, and this post went, briefly, to John Russell. Naturally Palmerston would have liked the Foreign Office, but he had had enough of a year's political tight-rope walking, and, after all, as to the Foreign Secretaryship 'j'y ai été, as the Frenchman said of foxhunting'.

He chose, instead, the Home Office, which at least gave him the political power he enjoyed so much, and comforted himself with the reflection that 'It does not do for a man to pass his whole life in one department, and the Home Office deals with the concerns of the country internally, and brings one in contact with one's fellow-countrymen, besides which it gives one more influence in regard to the militia and the defences of the country'.

So, in the last week of 1852, Palmerston went to Windsor with his new colleagues to receive their seals of office, where Prince Albert noted that he looked ill and walked on two sticks, and the Queen later wrote to her Uncle Leopold that her new Home Secretary was 'terribly altered, and all his friends think him breaking'. Although Palmerston had many years to go before he broke, it was certainly true he had aged rapidly by the end of 1852. Of course, he was sixty-eight years of age and had been tormented with gout for some time, which undoubtedly rendered his traditionally jaunty step somewhat less jaunty. He had also suffered an illness during the early winter weeks and stayed away from the Commons on account of it.

These manifestations of advancing years did little to impair Palmerston's zest as Home Secretary. He set about mastering the details of his new department with the same enthusiasm he had once lavished on foreign affairs. Lord Shaftesbury, indeed, was later to pay him the handsomest of compliments when he said: 'I have never known any Home Secretary equal to Palmerston for readiness to undertake every good work of kindness, humanity, and social good, especially to the child and the working class. No fear of wealth, capital, or election-terrors; prepared at all times to run a-tilt if he could do good by it. Has already done more than ten of his predecessors.'

Shaftesbury, with his intimate family links with Palmerston and his commitment to industrial reform, was, of course, remarkably well-placed to influence the new Home Secretary. Not that Palmerston always went far enough to please Shaftesbury and the reformers: his 1853 Factory Act, for example, failed to cut the working hours of women and males under the age of eighteen from 60 to $57\frac{1}{2}$ hours per week, even though it prohibited all work by minors between 6 pm and 6 am. Palmerston also introduced the Truck Act, chiefly in response to the complaints of mine-workers and other working men who objected to being paid in goods and being compelled to buy supplies from shops owned by their employers.

Yet Palmerston was not invariably sympathetic to the British working man, and when he introduced a Bill that confirmed the rights of trade unions to combine for legal purposes, he at the same time rejected the request to legalise peaceful picketing; the Bill did not, however, pass the House of Lords. Even as he shied away from peaceful picketing, the landowner and Tory in him found the Succession Duty proposed by the earnest and reforming Chancellor of the Excequer, William Ewart

Gladstone, too much to swallow and he querulously asked Lord Lansdowne: 'Suppose a man succeed to an estate giving a taxable income of £2,000 a year when his chances of life were 30 years; the value of his estate would be £60,000, 10 per cent on £60,000 would be £6,000, just equal to *Three times his income.*

'How much is such a man to pay? Is he to go to the Union House & hand over his Estate to the Treas[ury] till the amount is paid?'

But on many other issues Palmerston demonstrably moved with the times. In 1853 he introduced a Smoke Abatement Bill which did something to lift the pall of smoke and fog that so often enshrouded London and other Victorian cities. Brushing aside the objections that the Bill constituted an assault on the freedom of industrialists, he condemned the 'few, perhaps 100 gentlemen, connected with these different furnaces in London, who wished to make 2,000,000 of their fellow-inhabitants swallow the smoke which they could not themselves consume, and who thereby helped to deface all our architectural monuments, and to impose the greatest inconvenience and injury upon the lower class'. Of course Palmerston's reform did not clear the atmosphere of London at one stroke, and forty years later 'pea-souper' fogs could still swirl ominously round the deerstalker of Sherlock Holmes and envelop the hansom cabs of the metropolis.

One of Palmerston's great virtues as Home Secretary was his personal dedication to exercise and good health. Following in the medically progressive footsteps of his late father the second Viscount, he lent his support to a private member's bill to make vaccination against smallpox compulsory. He also believed that public health boards, with compulsory powers, should be established, and he took a practical view of the necessary means to prevent cholera epidemics, telling the Edinburgh Presbytery that:

... the Maker of the Universe has established certain laws of nature for the planet in which we live, and the weal or woe of mankind depends upon the observance or neglect of those laws. One of those laws connects health with the absence of those gaseous exhalations which proceed from over-crowded human beings, or from decomposing substances, whether animal or vegetable.... Lord Palmerston would, therefore, suggest that the best course which the people of this country can pursue to deserve that the further progress of the cholera should be stayed, will be to employ the interval that will elapse between the present time and the beginning of next spring in planning and executing measures by which those portions of their towns and cities which are inhabited by the poorest classes, and which, from the nature of things, must need purification and improvement, may be freed from those causes and sources of contagion which, if allowed to remain, will infallibly breed pestilence, and be fruitful in death, in spite of all the prayers and fastings of a united but inactive nation.

So forthright was this statement that it occurred to some that Lord Palmerston was treating Heaven as if it was a foreign power.

Palmerston also stirred up considerable controversy, again in the interests of public health, with his Act prohibiting the time-hallowed custom of burying notable members of society beneath the floors of churches and chapels. Undismayed by the protests of influential families and outraged ecclesiastics, Palmerston pushed the Bill through, blandly enquiring, 'why, pray, should archbishops and bishops and deans and canons be buried under churches if other persons are not to be so? What special connection is there between church dignities and the privilege of being decomposed under the feet of survivors? ... and as to burying bodies under thronged churches, you might as well put them under libraries, drawing-rooms and dining-rooms.'

Though not an advocate of total abstinence from alcohol, Palmerston was a moderate drinker who threw his official weight against the mid-Victorian beer-shops or public houses.

He particularly disapproved of drinking on the premises of the beer-shops and told William Gladstone in 1853 that 'The Beer Shops licensed to have the Beer drunk on the Premises are a Pest to the Community. They are Haunts of Thieves and Schools for Prostitutes. They demoralize the lower Classes. . . . The words "licensed to be drunk on the Premises" are by the common People interpreted as applicable to the Customers as well as to the Liquor.' His solution was 'to put down beershops, and let shopkeepers sell beer like oil and vinegar and treacle, to be carried home and drunk with wives and children'. In other words, Palmerston favoured the principle of off-licence sales of alcohol, and drinking bouts in the living-room rather than in the potentially iniquitous beer-shop. But he was no thoroughbred Puritan in these matters, and at the same time that he gave a fillip to the Temperance Societies he steadfastly refused to suppress betting.

The thorny problems of prison reform also exercised Palmerston's intelligence. The treatment of convicts was a matter for sharp public debate: on the one side there were those who considered that, despite transportation and the treadmill, prison conditions should be made more unpleasant; on the other, reformers wanted conditions to be improved and young offenders to be given a better chance of mending their ways.

Palmerston's record on penal reform was mixed. In the prisons under the control of the Home Office he reduced the maximum period to be spent in solitary confinement from eighteen to nine months. In the eyes of mid-nineteenth-century progressives, however, this amounted to a retrogressive step since it was reckoned that solitary confinement kept first offenders immune from the corrupting influences of hardened prisoners. In August 1853 Palmerston introduced the Penal Servitude Bill which ended the system of transportation for long-term prisoners to Van Diemen's Land (modern Tasmania). Instead of transportation the Bill substituted shorter terms of imprisonment in British jails, and also provided for model prisoners to be released on tickets-of-leave in Britain in order to take jobs outside of the penitentiaries. The die-hard opponents of this Act considered the ticket-of-leave system to be too soft, and Palmerston was urged to make prison conditions, including the food, less agreeable.

Through Lord Shaftesbury's influence, Palmerston became especially interested in the treatment of juvenile offenders. As a result of Shaftesbury's campaigning, which had revealed that there were almost twelve thousand young prisoners under the age of seventeen in British prisons, a separate penitentiary at Parkhurst on the Isle of Wight had been opened before Palmerston became Home Secretary. Palmerston, however, went further than this in 1854 when he brought in the Reformatory Schools Act which allowed young offenders to be transferred from prison to reformatory schools. He also backed the work of Shaftesbury's Prisoners' Aid Society, which aimed at helping released convicts find suitable work. In 1854, moreover, he was responsible for persuading the Queen and the Cabinet to pardon the Irish nationalist and Chartist prisoners still in Van Diemen's Land on condition that they did not re-enter Britain; but this move was not pure philanthropy on Palmerston's part, since there was widespread sympathy, both in Australia and the United Kingdom, for these political prisoners.

Though the Radicals could applaud the release of the political prisoners from Van Diemen's Land, many were shocked by Palmerston's handling of accusations that Kossuth, the celebrated Hungarian nationalist leader, was plotting to manufacture arms in Britain, in collaboration with a sympathetic British manufacturer, and send them to Hungary. There proved to be no legal case against Kossuth, but his British supporters accused Palmerston of allowing plain-clothes policemen to keep a close watch on foreign political refugees.

Palmerston denied that the Austrian government had persuaded the British authorities to trail potential plotters, but the impression remained that foreign refugees were being subjected to surveillance and harassment.

On the whole Palmerston's tenure at the Home Office was astonishingly progressive for a man nearing seventy with no previous experience of domestic administration. His readiness to increase government interference in a wide range of fields was particularly surprising from a believer in the principles of Political Economy as dispensed by Professor Stewart of Edinburgh. Most authorities believed that the government should intervene hardly at all in the economy. If hours of work were reduced, output would fall, British goods would be undersold by foreign products and mass unemployment would result. The great thing about Palmerston was that he had very few absolute prejudices; he was prepared to change his mind in the light of new evidence. At the beginning of the century few members of the governing classes had any idea of the real conditions in which the vast majority of their fellow subjects spent their lives. The slender evidence available seemed to justify the assumptions of the *laissez faire* school. Since then the appalling revelations of Chadwick's 'Report on the Sanitary Condition of the Labouring Classes' and Shaftesbury's 'Report on Mines' had made Palmerston reject his earlier axioms. Conditions were so deplorable that something had to be done.

Palmerston was also open to arguments of efficiency. Squalor and misery might drive the working class to revolution, yet such conditions were not even good for the economic well-being of the country. A man with proper rest and reasonable health might produce as much in a short time as a tired and sick man in a fourteen-hour day. Above all, if Britain was to set herself up as the moral arbitrator of the world, the model for less fortunate nations to follow, then she must make sure that the condition of her own people was an advertisment for the British way of life.

Palmerston's period as Home Secretary did a great deal to reinstate him in the good opinions of Queen Victoria and Prince Albert, and Lady Palmerston noted with pleasure that they were 'very friendly and courteous now to P. as in olden times'. In the autumn of 1853 he was invited to Balmoral. Lady Palmerston, though she complained that Broadlands was 'shorn of its beams' by his departure, gave him some good advice: 'Don't shut yourself up too much with your papers in your distant room. But remember you have only one week to remain there, so you should manage to make yourself agreeable and to appear to enjoy the society.'

It seems that Palmerston succeeded in following his wife's advice, which was just as well, for in the Near East events were unfolding that were to take him to the premiership within eighteen months. During 1853 both the Tsar of Russia and the French Emperor Napoleon III asserted their claims to protect the Greek Orthodox and Roman Catholic subjects of the Turkish Sultan respectively, and also quarrelled over which religious order was to oversee the Holy Places in Palestine. In particular the Tsar (who had already diagnosed Turkey as 'the sick man of Europe') was pressing for a measure of control over the Turkish administration. The Turks naturally resisted these demands. If Russia and Turkey went to war it was likely that the Tsar's armies would make rapid headway and that the great port of Constantinople, the symbolic key to the Eastern Mediterranean, would fall into Russian hands. This was a prospect that had haunted British and French foreign policy-makers for a considerable time, and they were not prepared to see it happen.

Though Home Secretary, Palmerston was deeply involved in the deepening crisis in the Near East and the Balkans. His preoccupation with these matters was nicely illustrated when an anxious Queen sent for him to enquire about strike troubles in the North of England. 'Pray, Lord Palmerston,' she asked, 'have you any news?' 'There is no definite news, Madam', he replied, 'but it seems certain that the Turks have crossed the Danube.'

Lord Aberdeen, the prime minister, who believed that the Turks had no business in Europe anyway, was not inclined to take a bellicose approach to Russian pressures on the Sultan. But his views were not shared by a large section of the press and many members of the British public who wanted to contain Russian expansion; nor were they shared by Palmerston. Unfortunately, since Palmerston did not have control of foreign affairs, he tried to assert his views by influencing Aberdeen's policy and by whipping up anti-Russian feeling in the country through, for example, writing editorials for the *Morning Post.*

There is no doubt that there was a widespread feeling in the country that Palmerston should be the man dealing with the Russians, and Prince Albert wrote somewhat apprehensively to his confidant, Baron Stockmar, 'the Palmerstonian stocks have gone up immensely, people saying that if he had been at the Foreign Office, he would by his energy have brought Russia to reason'. Certainly there is every reason to believe that Palmerston would have stood a good chance of averting war by his usual mixture of firmness and moderation. Since he was removed from the control of foreign affairs, however, his advice was more unyielding than it might otherwise have been, and he expressed a strong desire to 'make an Example of the Red-haired barbarians'.

In May 1853 the Russians were poised to invade the provinces of Moldavia and Wallachia (now part of modern Romania). The French fleet was ready to sail to the Dardanelles, but the British fleet was at first kept back after Palmerston and John Russell had been overruled in Cabinet. Palmerston was convinced that 'the Policy and Practice of the Russian Government in regard to Turkey and Persia has always been to push forward its encroachments as fast and as far as the apathy or want of Firmness of other Governments would allow it to go, but always to stop and retire when it has met with decided Resistance.... if England and France make the Russian Government clearly understand that the Russian troops *must* go out, the Russian Government will somehow or other find the way to make them go out'.

Palmerston and Russell did eventually persuade the Cabinet to send the Royal Navy to the Dardanelles, upon which the Tsar invaded Moldavia and Wallachia in the summer of 1853. Palmerston now proceeded to promote anti-Russian feeling with all the means at his command; in the process he actively undermined the government's attempt to find a diplomatic solution to the situation. In October 1853 Turkey declared war on Russia, to much popular enthusiasm in Britain; among those who rejoiced at the news were Alfred Tennyson, Charles Kingsley and the exiled Karl Marx. There were even voices in the streets that sang of Prince Albert:

> Little Al, the royal pal,
> They say has turned a Russian.

And a general dislike of foreign meddlers was expressed in the verse:

> Bad luck, they say, both night and day,
> To the Cobugs and the humbugs,
> The Witermbugs and the Scarembugs,
> And all the German horserugs;
> And the old bug of Aberdeen,
> The Peterbugs and Prussians.
> May Providence protect the Turks
> And massacre the Russians.

In many ways the situation presented another instalment of the Eastern Crisis of 1840 which brought England and France close to war. Palmerston still believed that the Ottoman Empire must be preserved to guard against Russian expansion - however unpleasant its rule and however corrupt its administration.

Things were simpler than they had been in 1840. The French had previously tried to break up the Ottoman Empire for their own local advantage, regardless of the wider consequences. Now they had seen sense, but Palmerston too had changed. The 1848 Revolution had shown the weakness of political stability in France, yet it was obviously in Britain's interest that things should be reasonably quiet across the Channel. There was now an Empire in France, potentially expansionist, but better than anarchy. The best way to contain French ambition was to act in concert with her and allow her the prestige of a successful war which would improve the Emperor's standing with his own countrymen. Palmerston's views in 1854 were not that unlike those advanced by his enemies in 1840.

In the midst of feverish speculations, Palmerston threatened to resign from the Cabinet over a proposal of Lord John Russell to extend the franchise to some working-class males resident in towns. He wrote angrily to Lord Aberdeen that 'I do not chuse to be dragged through the dirt by John Russell'. While Aberdeen debated his course of action, the Russians annihilated a Turkish squadron at Sinope. Palmerston then proceeded to resign in earnest, and the nation assumed that the real issue of contention was the government's appeasement policy towards Russia.

But a week later, having reaped the rewards of his resignation, Palmerston was back in the Cabinet, having sent Aberdeen a 'grumpy and ungrammatical' note of peace. The nation, however, was on the brink of war and the efforts of John Bright's Peace Society were of no avail. In March 1854, Britain and France declared war against Russia, though it was to be September before the Allied armies landed in the Crimea.

Indeed the Cabinet at first had no clear idea as to how or where to strike at Russia, though in March Palmerston, from the inappropriate confines of the Home Office, was urging 'the advantage of a great attack on the Crimea'. This was eventually the strategy decided upon; the vital Russian naval base of

Sebastopol would be taken and the Russian government forced to agree to the Allied peace terms. Palmerston was jauntily optimistic over the prospect, claiming that 'sixty thousand English and French troops, with the fleets co-operating, would accomplish the object in six weeks after landing, and if this blow was accompanied by successful operations in Georgia and Circassia, we might have a merry Christmas and a happy New Year'.

Unfortunately the Anglo-French armies led by Lord Raglan and Marshal St Arnaud (soon to be succeeded by General Canrobert) did not sweep on to Sebastopol. Instead they slogged their way crudely and inefficiently, if occasionally gloriously, to the gates of the citadel, via Pyrrhic engagements at the Alma, Balaclava and Inkerman. The freezing Crimean winter clamped down on the trenches around Sebastopol, but not before the ravages of cholera and typhoid, the muddles on the battlefield, and the scandalous deficiencies in supply and medical treatment had outraged British public opinion.

The New Year of 1855 was far from happy, and the government became very unpopular. A move to replace the Duke of Newcastle as Secretary for War with Palmerston failed; in January 1855 Russell resigned from the Cabinet in protest against the management of the war. On 25 January the Radical MP, John Roebuck, moved a resolution demanding a Parliamentary Committee of Inquiry into the conduct of the war; Russell supported the motion, and Palmerston spoke half-heartedly, as a member of the government, against it. Roebuck's motion was carried by 305 votes to 157, an embarrassingly large margin. The Cabinet resigned, and the search for a new prime minister began. Lord Derby was quite sure that it could not be Palmerston whom he considered 'very deaf as well as very blind . . . seventy-one years old, and . . . in fact, though he still kept up his sprightly manners of youth, it was evident that his day was gone by'. Events, however, were to prove Lord Derby to be ludicrously mistaken.

7

THE INEVITABLE MAN: PRIME MINISTER
1855-8

THOUGH THE MOOD of the country made Palmerston, as he himself acknowledged, the inevitable man for the premiership, he did not step promptly and blithely into supreme office on Aberdeen's resignation. Queen Victoria was not anxious to ask him to form an administration until she had exhausted other possibilities. In any case, it was her constitutional duty to ask Lord Derby, as leader of the opposition, to form a government. Derby secured Palmerston's agreement to serve under him at the War Office but only on condition that Lord Clarendon remained Foreign Secretary; since Clarendon hated Derby it proved impossible to fulfill this condition, and the attempt at Cabinet-making collapsed.

The Queen still would not send for Palmerston. She asked Lord Lansdowne and then Lord Clarendon to form an administration, but they both declined to do so. She then turned to Lord John Russell, with the discreet comment that 'it would give her particular satisfaction if Lord Palmerston would join this formation'. Palmerston made clear his willingness to serve under Russell - indeed, with his usual thirst for office, he was apparently willing to serve under any prime minister. However, Russell's late colleagues, particularly the Peelites, were less enthusiastic for his leadership after his attacks on the conduct of the war and refused point-blank to join his prospective administration. When Palmerston saw that Lord Clarendon was determined not to take the Foreign Office under Russell, he too declared his unwillingness to serve. As her elder statesmen whirled waspishly and coquettishly around her, Victoria complained: 'Lord John Russell may resign, and Lord Aberdeen may resign, but I *can't* resign. I sometimes wish I could.'

But on 4 February 1855, Palmerston was summoned to Buckingham Palace and invited to form a government. His most difficult task lay in persuading the leading Peelites – the Duke of Argyll, William Gladstone and Sidney Herbert – to serve under him, since they felt that by so doing they would be betraying their leader Aberdeen. To his credit, Aberdeen, who had decided to retire from public life, urged his three colleagues to join Palmerston, and eventually they agreed. By the evening of 5 February Palmerston was able to announce that he had formed his first administration: Lord Clarendon remained Foreign Secretary and Gladstone Chancellor of the Exchequer; the Whig Lord Panmure became Secretary of State for War, and Sidney Herbert took the newly-created office of Secretary for the Colonies; Sir George Grey became Home Secretary and the Duke of Argyll Postmaster-General. Palmerston tried to bring his Conservative but reforming son-in-law, Lord Shaftesbury, into his Cabinet as Chancellor of the Duchy of Lancaster, but the Whigs objected and a relieved Shaftesbury turned once more to his humanitarian activities.

So Palmerston was now prime minister at the age of seventy, and the British nation breathed a general sigh of relief that the conduct of the war lay in his hands. On 17 February *Punch* caught the public mood in a cartoon showing a prize-fighting set-to between 'Pam, the Downing Street Pet' and 'The Russian Spider'. The acclaim, however, was not universal. The Radical John Bright wrote angrily and uncharitably in his journal, 'Palmerston Prime Minister. What a hoax! The aged charlatan has at length attained the great object of his long and unscrupulous ambition . . . it passes my comprehension how the country is to be saved from its disasters and disgraces by a man who is over seventy years of age, who has never been known to do anything on which a solid reputation can be built.' Bright's fellow-Radical Richard Cobden wrote scathingly and a little inaccurately 'all men of the age of seventy-two [sic], with unsatisfied ambitions, are desperadoes'.

Disraeli, without office in 1855, told Lady Londonderry that though Palmerston was 'really an imposter, utterly exhausted, and at the best only ginger-beer, and not champagne, and now an old painted pantaloon, very deaf, very blind, and with false teeth, which would fall out of his mouth while speaking if he did not hesitate and halt so in his talk, here is a man which the country resolves to associate with energy, wisdom and eloquence, and will until he has tried and failed'. Disraeli exaggerated Palmerston's physical ailments and senility. Though it was true that he wore ill-fitting false teeth, refused to rely on spectacles, limped from gout, and sometimes fell asleep in Cabinet or on the Treasury Bench, he was still capable of extraordinary feats of endurance and hard work. Rigorous exercise continued to be his god, and whenever possible he undertook long walks, and rode to hounds when at Broadlands.

Palmerston had been in Parliament for forty-eight years before he was called upon to direct the affairs of the nation. How had he managed to climb to the top of the 'greasy pole'? It is unlikely that he would have succeeded if the country had not been at war. Aberdeen was perfectly capable of running a successful peacetime government, he was strongly supported by the Queen and Prince Albert and was generally respected as the heir to the traditions of Robert Peel. Palmerston must have been well aware that war, the first since 1815, would give him his chance. It would be unfair to say that he cynically pushed the country into war in order to promote his own political career; but his newspaper articles certainly inflamed public opinion which in turn pushed on a reluctant government.

Aberdeen was in a difficult position. He was known to have been lukewarm about going to war; when things went wrong it was easy for people to say that he was only playing at war and was half-hearted in his will to win. But if Aberdeen was deposed, why should Palmerston be his inevitable successor? War tended to bring out patriotic fervour and since it was the Tories who traditionally claimed to be the patriotic party, a government minority headed by Lord Derby and Disraeli could have been expected. Yet the Tory party was not the party of patriotism in the 1850s; these were years when Disraeli could talk of colonies as 'wretched burdens'. The Tory failure to exploit its traditional advantage may be one of the reasons for the party's poor performance at the mid-nineteenth century polls. What Palmerston had done was to steal the Tories' clothes; instead of being an attribute of the Right, patriotism came to be associated with the Left for a few years.

But if the premiership had been decided by the personal preference of Whig MPs it is still likely that Russell rather than Palmerston would have followed Aberdeen. Despite Russell's occasional lapses, he was a Whig to the very core of his being, whereas there was always a doubt about Palmerston. Palmerston was imposed on reluctant politicians by the country at large. Very few other men had enjoyed this distinction – notably William Pitt the Elder in the Seven Years' War and the Younger in 1783. The public mood just would not accept a government other than one headed by Henry Temple, Viscount Palmerston. Various reasons have been suggested earlier to explain why Palmerston was drawn to the people but why was the attraction mutual?

Palmerston was certainly not a man who could inspire unbounded enthusiasm whenever he opened his mouth. As an

119

orator Palmerston was unpredictable; sometimes he was outstanding, sometimes his performances were lamentable. His style was developed for Parliament, not for mass audiences. The idea of stumping around the country and addressing huge crowds, as later party leaders were to do, would have struck Palmerston as unpardonably vulgar. Palmerston's political manner was anything but cosy; he certainly needed publicity to get his message over to the people but, if television had existed in 1855, it is very unlikely that Palmerston would have gone to Downing Street.

Palmerston became prime minister not for what he really was but for what people thought he was. He was quite prepared to maintain the illusion and this is where his contacts with the newspaper world came in so useful. In the 1850s newspapers did not even carry photographs; the word picture of Palmerston could diverge considerably from reality. The thing that people really admired was pluck - what was called 'bottom' in the eighteenth century - a certain wild recklessness personified by men who had staked their fortune on a cockroach race. The public thought that this was what Palmerston was doing in politics. They did not know just how well he had studied the form.

If a man had pluck it served him well. The middle classes might be appalled at risky politics but working men were becoming more influential in politics. Palmerston did not altogether welcome this development but he was quite prepared to profit from it. Prosperity at home meant that, even without a new Reform Bill, more people were meeting the requirements of the 1832 Act. Many of the new voters, and those who would soon be able to vote, probably saw national and even international politics in terms of a horse race or even a cock fight. The contestant who showed the greatest spirit was the one to cheer for. Apart from a few idealised engravings, ordinary people probably did not know what Palmerston looked like. In any case, they did not care whether he had false teeth, dyed side-whiskers, or the gout. They wanted a man to win the war for them; to give the Russians a drubbing and, if possible, keep the French from stealing the lion's share of martial glory. They felt that Britain's honour was safe with Palmerston and, overall, they were right. Palmerston had been cast in the role of national saviour; this must have caused him little surprise for he had, after all, been rehearsing the part for the past few years - now the call had come.

Palmerston's first trial in the House of Commons as prime minister was not, however, a striking success. Faced with Roebuck's resolution calling for a committee of inquiry into the war, he tried to emulate Richard II's appeal to the disaffected peasants during the great uprising of 1381, reminding the Commons that the young King had said ' "You have lost your leader, my friends; I will be your leader", so I should say to the House of Commons, if they will agree not to appoint this Committee, the Government will be their Committee.' But the MPs were unimpressed, and Palmerston acceded to the establishment of the committee. As a result he lost three of his four Peelites (Gladstone, Herbert and Sir James Graham) who would not accept the committee on constitutional grounds. Their resignation did not bring down Palmerston's government, and indeed gave him the opportunity to offer John Russell, who had been packed off to Vienna as British plenipotentiary to some lukewarm peace talks, the Colonial Office on his return from his mission.

This crisis surmounted, Palmerston plunged into the management of the war. The Allied armies were huddled around Sebastopol, where their numbers were soon to be swelled to 250,000 as foreign mercenaries and Sardinians sailed to the Crimea. Sebastopol, however, held out, while Palmerston busied himself with the details of weapons and ammunition, protective headgear, and the necessary cleanliness to keep cholera and typhoid at bay. Unfortunately a clean sweep was also needed of many of the army commanders and civil and military administrators of the war machine. Here Palmerston failed to carry out the appropriate corrective surgery: Lord Raglan, the British Commander-in-Chief, retained his position until he tactfully died in June 1855, succumbing (so Florence Nightingale believed) to a broken heart! His replacement General Simpson was, if anything, more ineffective still; but when Simpson was eventually persuaded to resign another nonentity, General Codrington, took his place.

Palmerston was similarly reluctant to sack the Secretary for War, Lord Panmure, despite his evident departmental incompetence. After all, Panmure was very rich and contributed generously to party funds. Palmerston did, however remove the controversial figures of General Airey, the Quartermaster-General, and General Estcourt, the Adjutant-General. Generally Palmerston failed to appreciate the crying need for wholesale army reform. He was prepared to improve matters of supply and service, but only to a limited extent. He resolutely refused to abandon flogging, pointing out that the British army's rank and file was composed chiefly of criminals. Nor did he take kindly to criticisms of the aristocratic stranglehold on commissions. Palmerston did not altogether support the system of purchasing commissions, but he expressed his belief that 'it was very desirable to connect the higher classes of society with the Army. . . . It was only when the Army was unconnected with those whose property gave them an interest in the country, and was commanded by unprincipled military adventurers, that it ever became formidable to the liberties of the nation.' So although Palmerston improved the deplorable transport and supply services of the army, the blood of the officer class continued to be of the purest blue.

Palmerston was quite right to argue that there was no reason why an officer should not be both aristocratic and competent. After all, the prime minister managed to combine the two qualities very satisfactorily. Of course there were serious deficiencies, but one should not assume that nineteenth-century armies would have been better for the application of twentieth-century principles. Many of the urban Radicals who talked of making the army more democratic had no idea of the realities of military life. The fact remained that the best training for a cavalry officer was to learn his horsemanship as a boy in the hunting field. It was a training that the middle classes did not have.

As the war dragged ingloriously towards its end, the Emperor Napoleon III and the Empress Eugénie came to Britain in April 1855. Despite her sympathy for the deposed Louis Philippe, and her early suspicions of the new Emperor of the French, Queen Victoria was quite captivated by the charm of the Imperial couple. The Emperor celebrated his birthday by a drive to see the Crystal Palace – where the fountains, in an anti-gallic fit, refused to work. The British public, however, were positively pro-French as a result of the war and of Napoleon III's visit in the guise of a benevolent and martial ally. Palmerston's dealings with Napoleon III were of necessity more businesslike. In particular, he dissuaded the Emperor from his grand project of taking personal command of the French forces in the Crimea. Not only would such a foray have awoken uncomfortable memories of another, greater Bonaparte, but it would have given France an unfair advantage since Victoria, for all her desire to give the Russians 'such a beating', could hardly take command of her forces in the field.

Palmerston had other differences with France in 1855. He was concerned at the project of Ferdinand de Lesseps to cut a canal through the Suez isthmus. Though the proposed canal would benefit British commerce by providing a shorter route to the East, and would bring British India nearer, Palmerston feared that through the Suez Canal Company France would exert undue influence over Egypt. Though he raised a number of technical objections to the canal (not all of them worthy of serious attention), his real fears were diplomatic: 'It was natural that the Partisans of French Policy should consider it an object of great Importance to detach Egypt from Turkey in order thereby to cut off the easiest Channel of Communication between England and British India . . . to interpose between Syria and Egypt the Physical Barrier of a wide and deep Canal defended by military works, and the political Barrier of a strip of sand extending from the Mediterranean to the Red Sea granted away to, and occupied by a Company of Foreigners.' Palmerston's fears that Egypt would become 'a dependency of France' were in the event unrealised, and in 1882 British forces invaded the country and remained in occupation of the canal zone until 1955.

But it was not only the canal project that put strain on Anglo-French relations. The peace negotiations for ending the Crimean War also contained contentious issues. Preliminary negotiations had opened in Vienna at the start of 1855 but it was not until February 1856 that an armistice was signed and the Peace Congress proper began in Paris. Throughout these diplomatic manoeuvrings Palmerston held out for much harsher terms than Napoleon III was prepared to insist on. Indeed it was evident that the French Emperor had considerable sympathy for the new, reforming Tsar Alexander II, and was prepared to let him down lightly. Moreover, he had aspirations to aid Sardinia in liberating Italy from Austrian rule, and wanted an anti-Austrian alliance with Russia. Palmerston, who wanted to build up Austria as a barrier to Russian expansion, looked askance at these plans and even told the British plenipotentiary at the Paris peace talk (Lord Clarendon) that Britain would continue the war single-handed if her terms were not met. To bolster Clarendon's resolve, he reminded him on 28 February 1856 that 'Faint Heart never won Fair Lady'.

In the end, Palmerston did not get the settlement that he

wanted; this was chiefly due to Napoleon III, who told Clarendon that if the French people were obliged to continue the war until the hard British terms were met, then the aims of the war would have to be broadened to include the liberation of national groups (like the Italians and the Poles) at the expense of the Austrian and Russian empires. Palmerston shied away from the prospect of the Napoleonic eagle once more tearing the absolutist régimes of eastern Europe to shreds, and Britain subsequently modified her terms for peace. The final settlement left Russian territory intact, save for part of southern Bessarabia on the Danube's mouth, whereas Palmerston had advocated the cession of the Crimea and Circassia. Wallachia and Moldavia were united as an autonomous state (henceforth called Romania) under the nominal suzerainty of the Sultan; Palmerston was not happy with this union which he believed, rightly, would provide an awkward and belligerent neighbour for the Turks. But Britain had conceded these points in order to gain the vital Russian concession which involved the demilitarisation of the Black Sea except for a small number of light warships; the Russians undertook to demolish the naval facilities of Sebastopol, Odessa and two other ports. Although Russia reneged on this clause in 1870, the Peace of Paris that was signed on 30 March 1856 gave the Near East and the Turkish Empire two decades of security, and that, after all, had been the chief reason for Britain's involvement in the war.

As the cannons thumped in the London parks, and vast crowds gazed at the illuminations and celebrated the peace, Palmerston rode high in public estimation. He had brought the nation through an inglorious war to a not inglorious peace. Charles Greville, that avid retailer of gossip, even confessed that 'I myself, who for so many years regarded him politically with the greatest aversion and distrust, have come to think him the best minister we can have and wish him well'. Certainly it seemed as if the reign of Queen Victoria was to be matched by the reign of Lord Palmerston, with death the only usurper to be feared by either.

The domestic political scene was benign enough, though Palmerston faced defeat in the House of Commons on the unlikely issue as to whether or not military bands could play in the parks on Sunday afternoons. His son-in-law Shaftesbury, who was a passionate supporter of the proper observance of the Sabbath, invoked the Archbishop of Canterbury, and Palmerston gave way. But otherwise the Commons was quiet enough: the Tories were content that the war was won, and the Peelites were struggling to maintain their identity; Lord John Russell had left the Colonial Office, and was in Italy. Even the verbose and potentially awkward Gladstone was immersed in his library, and someone at Broadlands reported that the Chancellor was intent on restoring Helen of Troy's reputation, to which Lady Palmerston replied thoughtfully 'Well, you know people used to abuse Melbourne because he said Mary Magdalene was not near so bad as she was represented'.

Foreign affairs were not so agreeable as 1857 opened. Serious friction developed between Britain and the United States over the activities of an American adventurer, William Walker, in Nicaragua in Central America. Walker established himself as dictator of Nicaragua, and then seized Greytown in the neighbouring British protectorate of Mosquito. Palmerston was all for sending the Royal Navy to blockade Greytown, but his Cabinet colleagues persuaded him merely to send the fleet and not enforce a blockade. The incident provided a neat illustration of Palmerston's methods, in that he impulsively wished to send in the fleet, then listened to reason, and gave way to the objections (according to the Duke of Argyll) 'with the most perfect good humour. This was a great quality in a man so impulsive and strong-headed as he was, and so prone to violent action. It made him a much less dangerous man than he was supposed to be. But it was an all-important matter that he should have colleagues who understood him and were not afraid of him.'

Eventually the United States government dropped its support for Walker, and even sent a naval expedition to oust him from Nicaragua. Disagreements with the United States were not, however, at an end, and Palmerston was of the opinion that:

These Yankees are most disagreeable Fellows to have to do with about any American question; they are on the spot, strong, deeply interested in the matter, totally unscrupulous and dishonest and determined somehow or other to carry their Point; we are far away, weak from Distance, controuled by the Indifference of the nation as to the Question discussed, and by its strong commercial Interest in maintaining Peace with the United States . . . I have long felt inwardly convinced that the Anglo-Saxon Race will in Process of Time become Masters of the whole American Continent North and South . . . it is not for us to assist such a Consummation, but on the contrary we ought to delay it as long as possible.

Palmerston was also convinced that the Anglo-French honeymoon that had taken place in the Crimea could not last, though relations between the two countries remained friendly enough until the Orsini bomb plot of 1858. The prime minister, however, took a practical view of the future of Anglo-French affairs when he said:

It is quite evident that our marriage with France will soon end in a separation on account of Incompatibilité de moeurs; & it is mortifying & disgusting to find our dear friend the Emperor so little to be trusted. . . . After all, when we consider the different private interests of England & France, the different characters & habits of the two nations, we ought rather to be thankful at having got so much out of the Alliance, and at having maintained it so long than to be surprised or disappointed at its approaching end. It may still exist in name, and be useful to us for some purposes & on some occasions, but we must trust to our own Policy and to our own means for carrying us through the difficulties which from time to time we may have to deal with.

The year of 1857 saw British interests engaged further afield in

Asia. In the aftermath of the Crimean War, Persian forces laid seige to Herat, 'the gateway to India', in western Afghanistan. The British government were particularly sensitive to foreign influence in Afghanistan, and on this occasion had cause to believe that behind Persia stood the menace of expansionist Russia. At any rate, a British army invaded Persia in 1856, and early in 1857 inflicted a sharp and comprehensive defeat on their opponents. Palmerston subsequently made clear his wish for close and friendly cooperation between Britain and Persia, even though he had scant respect for the occupant of the Peacock Throne, declaring 'It is impossible to give the Shah the Garter, he is more deserving of the Halter'.

Even as British troops were dealing briskly with their Persian opponents, a further uncomfortable confrontation between East and West was taking place in China. The humiliating Treaty of Nanking in 1842 had been followed by a number of unpleasant incidents on the China coast between Britons and Chinese. Palmerston by no means automatically supported British citizens in these affrays, particularly if he considered them guilty of intemperate behaviour. At the same time he was determined to protect British interests. In 1847 he had written to Sir John Davis, the Governor of Hong Kong: 'We shall lose all the vantage ground we have gained by victories in China if we take a low tone. Of course we ought – and by we I mean all the English in China – to abstain from giving the Chinese any ground of complaint, and much more from anything like provocation or affront; but we must stop on the very threshold any attempt on their part to treat us otherwise than as equals and we must make them all clearly understand, though in the civilest terms, that our treaty rights must be respected. The Chinese must learn and be convinced that if they attack our people and our factories, they will be shot; and that if they ill-treat innocent Englishmen who are quietly exercising their treaty right of walking about the streets of Canton, they will be punished.'

Despite forthright, but not unreasonable, Palmerstonian tactics, and despite the overall willingness of the local Chinese authorities to cooperate with the British, a difficult situation developed in the autumn of 1856. The British authorities in Hong Kong allowed a liberal number of Chinese vessels trading with the island to register under the British flag. In October 1856 a small pirate vessel, the *Arrow*, flying the Union Jack, and nominally captained by an unseaworthy Ulsterman, was seized by Chinese coastguards. The authorities released the Ulsterman, but not the twelve Chinese pirates captured with him.

An incredible sequence of events now followed. Probably encouraged by the knowledge that Palmerston was in power at home, the Governor of Hong Kong, Sir John Bowring, and the British Consul at Canton, Harry Parkes, took a hard line with the Chinese authorities. They demanded, and eventually got, the release of the twelve pirates, despite their notoriety and the awkward fact that the British registration of the *Arrow* had expired some weeks before the vessel's capture. Bowring then pressed for an apology from the Chinese for insulting the British flag. When, understandably, he received no satisfaction on this point, the Royal Navy was ordered to bombard Canton, resulting in much loss of life and property.

As Canton burned and Britons were hunted down and beheaded by the Chinese mob, Palmerston told the Cabinet that they had no choice but to support Bowring in his clumsy but resolute stand. A storm broke about Palmerston's head in the House of Commons, where Tories, Peelites and Radicals harried the government. Cobden moved a vote of censure in March 1857, and Disraeli said, 'Let the noble Lord not only complain to the country, but let him appeal to the country. . . . I should like to see the programme of the proud leader of the Liberal party - "No Reform! New Taxes! Canton Blazing! Persia Invaded!" ' Palmerston, very low on account of gout and a bad cold, replied that if the House passed the vote of censure it would mean a vote to 'abandon a large community of the British subjects at the extreme end of the globe to a set of barbarians – a set of kidnapping, murdering, poisoning barbarians'.

But Palmerston caught only enough echoes of his Don Pacifico speech to reduce the opposition's majority to sixteen votes. He proceeded to ask a sympathetic Queen for a dissolution, and went to the country. His appeal was direct and powerful, and contained in his address to the loyal electors of Tiverton, where he insisted that 'an insolent barbarian, wielding authority at Canton [the Chinese governor], had violated the British flag'. In other words, Lord Palmerston, Jack Tar and the British Lion (not to speak of the powerful commercial interests trading with the Far East) needed the electorate to back them up. The electorate showed itself enthusiastic to do just that. The election results were a resounding triumph for Palmerston and doom for his opponents: Bright and Cobden lost their seats, and Palmerston now enjoyed a comfortable Commons majority of 85 over the opposition; he towered above his political enemies, the Queen was anxious for his health, and Lord Shaftesbury wrote with quasi-religious fervour 'P's popularity is wonderful – strange to say, the whole turns on his name'. With his thumping majority under his belt, Palmerston proceeded to conclude the *Arrow* War at leisure, wringing compensation and further concessions from the Chinese by force of arms.

As the pall of smoke hung over Canton, British India was seized by the strange convulsion of the great Mutiny of 1857-9. The roots of the Mutiny went deep. The territorial annexations and reforming tendencies of the East India Company had affronted many sections of Indian society in the half-century since the victorious conclusion of the Maratha Wars in 1818 had unquestionably established the British as the paramount power in the subcontinent. For the vast majority of the Indian people it was probably irrelevant whether the Mogul Emperor, the Maratha Confederacy or the Honourable East India Company ruled them; the timeless struggle for subsistence was their overwhelming preoccupation. Peasant India, fatalistic and passive, was an unlikely recruiting ground for bloodstained revolutionaries.

Princes, landlords, religious leaders, and members of the upper reaches of Hindu and Muslim society saw things differently. The East India Company had toppled Indian rulers, dispossessed landlords, and had seemed to encourage attacks on the indigenous religious and cultural order. The proselytising of evangelical Christian missionaries, the abolition of *suttee* (the burning of Hindu widows) and the passing of laws permitting the remarriage of such widows, the attempt to stamp out the Thugs, who robbed and strangled travellers as sacrifices to the goddess Kali, all seemed to be part of the Company's programme to subvert the Indian tradition.

The governor-generalship of Lord Dalhousie (1848-56) intensified the resentments that had been building up for many years. Dalhousie confidently asserted the paramountcy of the Company, thus also implying the superiority of British ways over Indian. His plans to improve road and rail communications were justified in terms of military security, but seemed further, perturbing examples of change to Indian traditionalists. Above all, Dalhousie's unashamed policy of territorial annexation was bound to alienate fallen rulers and their followers. As the climax to his series of annexations, Dalhousie brought the ancient province of Oudh under the Company's rule in 1856. Oudh, rich, fertile and densely populated, was the last great independent quasi-province in northern India. It lay between Bengal and the Punjab, straddling the grand trunk road from Calcutta to Delhi, the Ganges and the Jumna rivers, and the newly completed railway link between Allahabad and Cawnpore. In 1837 the Company had guaranteed the province's independence, but Dalhousie's annexation in 1856 was justified on the not unreasonable grounds of endemic civil disorder. A more compelling justification was that Oudh had become an anachronistic obstacle to the Company's plans for territorial and military aggrandisement throughout the whole of the Ganges valley.

The significance of the annexation of Oudh lay not only in its strategic importance, but also in the fact that 40,000 sepoys (nearly a third of the total) in the Army of Bengal had been recruited from the province. The East India Company maintained three armies, those of Bengal, Madras and Bombay. At the beginning of 1857 there were 45,522 European troops in India, consisting of four regiments of cavalry, thirty-one regiments of infantry and sixty-four batteries of artillery – some of which had Indian personnel. There were 232,224 sepoys serving in the three armies, of which 151,000 composed the Army of Bengal.

In general, the sepoys of the Bengal Army were drawn from the more exalted sections of Indian society: Brahmins and Rajputs if they were Hindus, of good-class Muslim families if followers of Islam. On donning their uniforms they did not become mere tools of Company policy; they maintained their religion, their caste, and their family connexions. Their unbroken links with their families had a twofold significance: one was that they were particularly sensitive to any fears or resentments that affected their families; the other was that they had an important status to maintain in the eyes of their relatives. Any slight to their religion, any threat to their caste or standing, would have resulted in rejection by family and friends.

The fifty years before the Mutiny had seen other military insurrections. In 1806 and 1824 sepoys had feared that the Company was undermining their religions; both mutinies had been ferociously suppressed. As late as 1852, a regiment had refused service in Burma, since crossing the sea would have involved its Hindu troops in a loss of caste; this regiment had been simply diverted to other duties. But early in 1857 dark rumours began to circulate concerning the issue of a new cartridge.

The Company had decided to equip its sepoy regiments with the Enfield rifle in place of the smooth-bored 'Brown Bess' musket. The rifle barrel of the new weapon necessitated a greasing of the cartridges in order to ram home easily the rifle bullet that was placed in the base of each cartridge. The loading procedure for these new 'balled' cartridges was as follows: first tear off the top of the cartridge; then pour the gun-powder down the rifle barrel; finally ram the empty container with its bullet down the rifle. It seems clear that between 1847 and 1857 there had been a wholesale change-over to 'balled' cartridges. Hitherto the 'unballed' cartridges had simply been thrown away, and the bullet taken from a separate pouch.

The fateful implication of this military change was that the sepoys came to believe that the grease on the cartridges was made from animal fat. To the Hindu the cow was a sacred animal, the Muslim believed that contact with the unclean pig would defile him. In January 1857 sepoys near the great Dum-Dum arsenal close to Calcutta became convinced that the new-issue cartridges were coated with cow and pig fat. Their suspicions seem to have been well-founded. That such a thing could happen indicates either blind stupidity or gross negligence on the part of the military authorities. Frederick Roberts, who fought against the Mutiny and won the Victoria Cross, and was later to become Field Marshal Lord Roberts of Kandahar, subsequently wrote: 'The cartridge was actually composed of the objectionable ingredients cow's fat and pig's lard; an incredible disregard of the sepoy's religious prejudices was displayed in the manufacture of these cartridges.'

In May 1857 the cartridge controversy resulted in a serious uprising at Meerut; Delhi fell, and the valley of the Ganges from West Bengal to the Punjab was the scene of mutiny and massacre. Cawnpore capitulated and Lucknow was hard-pressed. Small numbers of British troops and loyal sepoys fought hard to dislodge the mutineers, who, though numerically superior, often lacked coordinated leadership and a common set of aims. As the British regained lost ground they brought a whirlwind of reprisal and revenge in their wake.

Palmerston was at first accused of failing to take the uprising sufficiently seriously, and Lord Clarendon complained that 'confidence and courage are fine things . . . but they are bad when, as with Palmerston, they lead to neglect of the means of which success can be attained'. This was not altogether fair, since Palmerston eventually sent more than adequate reinforcements to India, and, in any case, by the end of the summer, the back of the Mutiny had been broken, chiefly by the exertions of the East India Company troops on the spot. Still, there was some justification for Clarendon's further, somewhat surprised, judgement that '[Palmerston] has a jolly way of looking at disasters'.

As the Mutiny abated, Palmerston was faced with the choice as to whether to support the Governor-General of British India, Lord Canning, in his policy of clemency, as opposed to indiscriminate revenge, towards the mutineers. After hesitating for some months to commit himself, Palmerston eventually came down on the side of 'Clemency Canning', thus earning the Governor-General's profound gratitude. Palmerston also decided to dismantle the political authority of the East India Company and transfer the administration of British India to the Crown instead. This was given effect in the 1858 Government of India Act.

The Act passed its third reading in the Commons in February 1858. But though Palmerston's stock stood high in the country as the man who put haughty Chinese and murderous sepoys firmly in their proper places, he was in fact only a few days from being overthrown as prime minister. The crisis arose out of the Orsini bomb plot. On 14 January an Italian nationalist named

Orsini threw a bomb at the carriage of the Emperor Napoleon III and the Empress Eugénie; neither was hurt, but several spectators were killed. It was subsequently revealed that Orsini had close links with Italian refugees in London, and that the explosives for the bomb had been manufactured in Britain. French protest flowed into London. Palmerston went out of his way to placate the French authorities by ordering the introduction of a Conspiracy to Murder Bill, which made it a felony to plot in Britain to murder anyone abroad. On the second reading of the Bill, however, the Radicals Milner-Gibson and Bright (now back in the Commons) moved an amendment criticising Palmerston for apparently kow-towing to the French ambassador's protests after the Orsini incident.

Palmerston reacted hastily to this amendment, though understandably outraged at the suggestion that he had meekly surrendered to French pressure. He adamantly denied that the Bill constituted a threat to the right of asylum for peaceable political refugees in Britain. Then, shaking his fist at Milner-Gibson, he accused him of previously advocating 'a policy of submission – of crouching to every foreign power with which we had any differences to discuss'. The Radicals were indignant, the Peelites unimpressed, and the astute Disraeli (having supported the Bill during its first reading ten days before) led the Conservatives into the division lobby against Palmerston. The amendment was carried by nineteen votes. Three days later, having endured the unaccustomed indignity of being hooted at in Regent's Park, Palmerston resigned, and Lord Derby formed a Conservative government – though one dangerously dependent upon Radical, Peelite and disaffected Whig support.

8

OLD PAM: PRIME MINISTER 1859-65

FOLLOWING HIS ABRUPT FALL from office, Palmerston saw no reason why he should be allowed to bounce back straightway into the premiership. In fact, he seemed determined to settle down to a prolonged period of Parliamentary opposition. The Prince Consort, like many humbler observers, was puzzled by the phenomenon:

A House of Commons, having been selected solely for the object, and on the ground of supporting Lord Palmerston personally (an instance in our Parliamentary history without parallel), holds him suddenly in such abhorrence, that not satisfied with having upset his Government, which had been successful in all its policy, and thrown him out, it will hardly listen to him when he speaks. . . . The man who was without rhyme or reason stamped the only English statesman, the champion of liberty, the man of the people, etc., etc., now, without his having changed in any one respect, having still the same virtues and the same faults that he always had, young and vigorous in his seventy-fifth year, and having succeeded in his policy, is now considered the head of a clique, the man of intrigue, past his work, etc., etc., – in fact hated!

Palmerston, however, set out to make the best that he could of the situation. He went out of his way to show himself a responsible opposition leader: he attended debates assiduously, criticised the government soundly, and even served on a

Parliamentary committee investigating the noisome subject of the pollution of the Thames. His wife, still outraged at his overthrow on 'merely a sham reason and an excuse by the Crafty to catch the fools', was confident that he would soon be swept back to power on the cry 'Palmerston and no base Coalitions'.

Unfortunately it was not quite as simple as that. The opposition to the Conservative government was fragmented. The Whigs and the Radicals now aspired to the title of Liberals; but there were Palmerstonian Liberals, John Russell Liberals and Cobdenite Liberals, not to speak of the Peelites clustered around William Gladstone. Although Lady Palmerston claimed that her husband retained 'a great affection for John [Russell]', there was no immediate prospect of a satisfactory fusion of the opposition groupings. It was a prospect that brought no small delight to Disraeli, who contentedly described 'a rumbling murmur, a groan, a shriek, distant thunder; and nobody knew whether it came from the top or the bottom of the House. There was a rent, a fissure in the ground. Then a village disappeared. Then a tall tower toppled down. And then the whole of the Opposition benches became one great dissolving view of anarchy!'

While in opposition Palmerston made good use of his unaccustomed leisure. In April 1858 he presided at a money-raising dinner for the Royal Literary Fund which gave financial assistance to impoverished authors. The Russian novelist Turgenev was there, and noted Palmerston's aristocratic deportment as well as his hard, oak-like face. The Palmerstons also entertained lavishly and informally at Broadlands, where meals were liable to be served at any time, and scandalous tales were told of Lord and Lady Palmerston's earlier love affairs. The United States Minister to Britain, George Dallas, was invited to Broadlands and was amazed to see Palmerston, who was then seventy-four, spend five vigorous hours on a pheasant shoot. Dallas was subsequently delighted to be able to beat Palmerston at billiards, a game at which the elder statesman by no means invariably triumphed – though he liked to bring off a dramatic shot or two if his wife was watching him!

In November Palmerston, accompanied by Lord Clarendon, visited Napoleon III at his palace at Compiègne. Palmerston had been in two minds as to whether to accept the Emperor's invitation: on the one hand, there was considerable anti-French feeling in Britain and Palmerston's political reputation might be damaged by the visit; on the other, it seemed foolish in the long term to offend Napoleon III by refusing his invitation. The upshot was that Palmerston and Clarendon decided that the political risks were worth taking, though in the event a large section of the British press attacked them for their visit.

Palmerston's trip to Compiègne had some colourful, not to say bizarre, qualities, though a female friend of Lord Clarendon was subsequently relieved that it did not include 'one of the riotous parties when ladies defend fortresses and mounds, and gentlemen pull them by the feet to make them lay down their arms, for your young companion P. would probably have joined in that fun too'. But there were festivities enough, even if at first it rained so hard that the guests had to play football in a gallery, and the Emperor demonstrated his horsemanship by prancing round with his lance in the riding school. When the weather cleared there was a curious shoot, with uniformed troopers beating the coverts for game, bugles sounding, and a decidedly Napoleonic and militarist flavour to the whole affair. Later on Palmerston donned his hunting pink for a stag chase in the pouring rain, assuring his concerned and muffled hosts that *'Rien ne perce un habit rouge'*.

Privately the Emperor talked to Palmerston at length on the subject of Italy, and told him that the best basis of the franchise was to confine it to married men (an interesting suggestion which would have had the effect of denying Palmerston the vote until the age of fifty-five). More privately still, Palmerston was deeply moved by the beauty of the Empress Eugénie, though much less moved by Napoleon's cousin, Princess Mathilde, whom he sat beside during dinner – noticeably preferring the food to her company.

On his return to Britain, Palmerston found Parliament much troubled by the problem of electoral reform. The Conservatives opposed a further extension of the franchise, and there were divisions within the Liberal ranks over the degree of reform desirable. Palmerston, in the recent past, had been far from sharing Bright's, or even Russell's, views on the need to reduce the £10 property qualification in the boroughs, and in 1857 had delivered himself of some markedly conservative opinions on the matter:

My Belief is that notwithstanding the slight stir got up about changes in our Representative System by a small minority here and there at the recent Elections the Country at large, including the Great Bulk of the Liberal Party, do not want or wish for any considerable changes in our Electoral System, and certainly do not wish for that particular change which the Radical Party cry out for, namely, the admission of a lower Class than the Ten Pounder . . . and I am decidedly of that opinion myself. . . .

Besides it must be remembered that changes in our Electoral System are not an End, but a Means to an End. Before 1830 there were a great many things in the State of our Laws which the Commercial & Manufacturing Communities wanted to have altered. . . . But almost all these things have now been altered. The Ends have been attained, & the Means now possessed have been found sufficient. . . . The men who wish for this are those who cannot sway the Intelligent & the Possessors of Property, and who think that they could wield for their own advantage the lower Classes whom they want to have let in to vote. . . .

My general notion is that votes might be given to officers of certain Ranks or perhaps of all Ranks in the Army & Navy, to all Barristers & Attorneys, to all graduates of universities, to all Medical Men registered as such & so on. I should be quite ready to give County votes to all occupiers of Houses rated Twenty Pounds; & it might be worth considering whether a man in a Borough changing from one house to another in that same Borough might not immediately retain his vote instead of waiting as I believe is now the case for a twelvemonth.

All this is a Bill of Fare that would fall far short of satisfying the appetite of our Radicals, but we must remember that we live under a Monarchy, fortunately for us, and if we intend that Monarchy should continue we should not run wild after Institutions and arrangements which essentially belong to that unhappy system of social organisation called a Republic.

But in March 1859 Palmerston was less dogmatic, and was able to support a rather unspecific motion of Russell's in the Commons calling for a reduction in the £10 property qualification in the boroughs. The motion was carried by 330 votes to 291 and the prime minister, Lord Derby, decided to go to the country. Apart from the issue of the extension of the franchise, a controversial problem of foreign policy was also put before the electorate. This centred on the decision of Napoleon III to invade Lombardy in support of the Italian nationalists' struggle against Austrian rule.

Palmerston seized the opportunity to outmanoeuvre John Russell for Radical support, and came down firmly on the side of France and the Italian nationalists. At his ritual appeal to the electors of Tiverton he declared himself, somewhat vaguely, in favour of reform, and then proceeded to spell out his Italian policy. Palmerston had already privately insisted that he was 'very Austrian north of the Alps, but very anti-Austrian south of the Alps', and that he would 'rejoice and feel relieved if Italy up to the Tyrol were freed of Austrian domination'. He said much the same thing at the Tiverton hustings, though insisting that Britain remain neutral.

The general election results did not produce a Conservative majority in the House of Commons, since there were now some 300 Conservative MPs to 350 of their opponents. Obviously if the opposition factions could combine they could form a government – but who was to lead that government? Palmerston and Russell were the two rivals for the premiership, and they bore each other grudges for past political wrongs. By June 1859, however, there had been enough groundwork done to enable the feuding factions to make a triumphant public demonstration of their fundamental accord. The meeting of 174 Liberal MPs took place at Willis's Rooms in St James Street, a particularly happy venue for Palmerston, since half a century before it had been Almack's Club where he had waltzed and flirted with Lady Cowper and Princess Lieven.

It was therefore appropriate that in June 1859 Palmerston should cap his former amorous triumphs with a resounding political achievement. He, Russell and Bright clasped each other's hands upon the platform at Willis's Rooms and pledged each other mutual support, and amid tumultuous cheers the modern Liberal party was, if not born, at least given a heartwarming baptism. Within the next few days the Liberal MPs came to the conclusion that Palmerston would serve them better as prime minister than Russell. It now remained to turn the government out.

On 11 June the government was defeated in the Commons on a vote of confidence. After an awkward hiatus, while the Queen asked Lord Granville to form an administration, Palmerston was charged with the same task. His exercise in Cabinet-making showed both the need to satisfy different factions and also the allurement which public office holds for most ambitious men. To satisfy faction he reluctantly gave John Russell the Foreign Office at the expense of Granville, and brought several Peelites into the Cabinet. But he was also able to lure Gladstone into his administration with the choice plum of the Chancellorship of the Exchequer, and even succeeded in appointing his bitter critic, Milner-Gibson, to the Presidency of the Board of Trade. Palmerston also made a determined attempt to include Richard Cobden in his government. Cobden wavered under the

141

influence of Palmerston's rancourless charm, but eventually said that he would not join unless Bright joined too. This Palmerston could not accept, in view of Bright's thundering attacks on the House of Lords; so Cobden and Bright stayed outside of the Cabinet, though agreeing to support the government in the House of Commons.

So 'Old Pam' entered upon his last premiership. His relations with his ministers, apart from Gladstone, were cordial enough, and he interfered surprisingly little in the detailed running of departmental affairs – even those of the Foreign Office – though he gave general directives on policy. Beyond the environs of Westminster and Whitehall his popularity was tremendous. His figure was still trim beneath his tight frock coat, and his hat was tilted more than a little. He rode from his home at Cambridge House on a grey horse down to Downing Street, where he sat among his colleagues like 'an old admiral cut out of oak, the figure-head of a seventy four gun ship in a Biscay squall'.

He was still remarkably healthy, staying on the Treasury benches for half the night if necessary, and (as the door-keeper of the Commons remarked) eating and sleeping on the premises. He hunted still, shot game when he could, and took a sporadic interest in horse-racing. In the last year of his life an observer saw him weaving deftly between the hansom cabs as he crossed Parliament Square. Once the Speaker of the House of Commons, fearing that he would catch cold by walking home so late at night, implored him to take a cab, to which Palmerston replied, 'Oh, I do indeed. I very often take a cab at night, and if you have both windows open it is almost as good as walking home.'

In his seventy-ninth year he was even cited as co-respondent in a much-talked-of divorce case. It was alleged in court that Palmerston had committed adultery with a Mrs O'Kane, the wife of an Irish Radical journalist. Palmerston denied the allegations, and Lady Palmerston treated them as a brazen attempt to extort money. Society was intrigued, the Nonconformist conscience was troubled, and in general people said that though the woman in question was Kane, was Palmerston Abel? Disraeli feared that the whole affair would merely enhance Palmerston's popularity, and wryly speculated that a general election was in the offing. O'Kane's case eventually collapsed; Palmerston was thus exonerated in the eyes of the virtuous, while less virtuous citizens chuckled and continued to believe the worst.

He was generally more amiable in his last years. He welcomed all the guests to Lady Palmerston's famous parties as if they were long-lost friends, even though he had often never clapped eyes on them before. He enquired tenderly after his one-time Chartist adversary Julian Harney, and even gave money in the lobby of the Commons to a collection for a Chartist leader. He was frequently extremely generous to his old political opponents, and offered them money, preferment and friendship. Of course, his concern was often compounded of political self-interest and spiced with condescension, but it was an effective weapon in his formidable armoury.

Palmerston's relationship with Queen Victoria positively blossomed during these years. Both the Queen and the Prince Consort took a far more favourable view of Palmerston as prime minister then they had as Foreign Secretary. There were of course differences of opinion, as when the Queen supported the Austrian and Palmerston the Italian cause in 1859, but it is clear that overall the relationship between monarch and prime minister was most harmonious. There were several reasons for this: one was that Palmerston had mellowed in the Indian summer of his life, and was more easily able at least to *appear* to consult the Queen closely on important matters; another was that he went out of his way to pay proper attention to Prince Albert, being instrumental in persuading Parliament to create him Prince Consort in 1857, and making complimentary references to him in public. These latter exercises in tact sometimes fell flat, as on the occasion of the Royal Literary

143

Fund dinner in 1858, for when Palmerston offered his audience the commonplace observation that the Queen enjoyed reading books he was greeted with loud cheers, but when he went on to remark that nobody could converse with Prince Albert without having his mind improved there was complete silence.

Palmerston also made great headway with Victoria by his sympathetic response to the Prince Consort's death from typhoid in 1861. Like his brother-in-law Melbourne twenty years before, Palmerston's eyes could fill with tears before the sharp and gratified gaze of his sovereign. No doubt his grief was genuine, though partly the response of an old man who loved life to the sudden death of a younger man. At any rate, he showed great interest in the project of a suitable memorial to Albert and favoured an open Grecian temple in Hyde Park containing 'a statue of the Prince Consort of heroic size'. He also took an interest in the moral welfare of the Prince of Wales (the future King Edward VII, telling Victoria that Bertie was 'the difficulty of the moment', and that he should marry as soon as possible. He proceeded gravely to warn Bertie (conveniently forgetting his own past escapades) against 'the allurements of fortune, position, and social temptation'. The Queen was appropriately grateful for this fatherly concern and 'would hardly have given Lord Palmerston credit for entering so entirely into my anxieties'.

So from Windsor to Westminster, and from Tiverton to Inverness, Palmerston's reputation rode high, and in 1861 *Punch* spoke for countless Britons when it saluted *John Palmerston*:

AIR – "John Highlandman"

An Irish Lord my John was born,
Both Dullness and Dons he held in scorn,
But he stood for Cambridge at twenty-one,
My gallant, gay, JOHN PALMERSTON!

Sing hey, my brisk JOHN PALMERSTON!
Sing ho, my blithe JOHN PALMERSTON!
Let Tory and Radical own they've none
To compare with my jaunty JOHN PALMERSTON.

Thanks to tact and temper, and taste for the trade,
For twenty years in office he stayed,
Let who would be Premier, it seemed all one,
So his Sec.-at-War was JOHN PALMERSTON.

Sing hey, &c.

There he did his work, for chief after chief,
Till the Tory party it came to grief;
And the Treasury Bench when the Whigs they won,
Who was Foreign Sec. but JOHN PALMERSTON!

Sing hey, &c.

Since then years thirty and one he's seen,
But no mark they've left on this evergreen;
Still the first in his place when Debate's begun,
And the last to leave it is PALMERSTON.

Sing hey, &c.

With his hat o'er his eyes, and his nose in the air,
So jaunty, and genial, and debonair
Talk at him – to him – against him – none
Can take a rise out of PALMERSTON.

Sing hey. &c.

And suppose his parish register say
He's seventy-seven, if he's a day;
What's that, if you're still all fire and fun
Like METHUSELAH, or JOHN PALMERSTON?

Sing hey, &c.

How to marshal a House of Commons fight,
How to punish DIZZY, or counter BRIGHT,
How Deputations ought to be done,
Who can teach so well as JOHN PALMERSTON?

    Sing hey, &c.

Agricultural meetings he holds by the ears,
Through their pacings puts Hampshire Volunteers,
Or with ROWCLIFFE takes up the gloves for fun,
This elderly evergreen, PALMERSTON.

    Sing hey, &c.

He'll resist the gale, or he'll bow to the storm--
He'll patronise BRIGHT, or he'll chaff Reform--
Make a Shafts'bury Bishop, or poke his fun
At original sin, will JOHN PALMERSTON.

    Sing hey, &c.

Of the Cinque-Ports, Warden he's made at last,
And fears of invasion aside are cast;
There's never a Mounseer son of a gun
Can come over you, my JOHN PALMERSTON--

    Sing hey, &c.

Since the days of the Patriarchs ne'er was seen
A head so grey with a heart so green;
And when, if ever, his day is done,
There'll be tears from Punch for JOHN PALMERSTON.

    Sing hey, &c.

Palmerston's last premiership began amid the stormy repercussions of the 1859 Italian crisis. Twenty days after his return to office the French and Austrian armies fought each other to a bloody standstill at Solferino in Lombardy. Horrified

146

by the carnage Napoleon III hastened to make peace with Austria, whereby Lombardy (but not Venetia) was ceded to Piedmont-Sardinia, while a few months later King Victor Emmanuel and Cavour were obliged to compensate France with Savoy and Nice. Palmerston did little in practice to aid the cause of Italian unification. Indeed, in 1860, fearing that the Italian patriot Garibaldi was a tool of Napoleon III and Cavour, he was inclined to prevent him crossing from Sicily to Naples with his small army of red-shirted liberators. Once Palmerston realised, however, that France was also contemplating stopping Garibaldi he adopted an attitude of strict neutrality. In the event, neither Britain nor France barred the redshirts' passage across the Straits of Messina; Garibaldi went on to conquer Naples for Piedmont-Savoy, and Palmerston, who had only at the last moment dropped his plan for intervention, was hailed by Italian nationalists as one of their foremost supporters.

Palmerston's domestic policies during 1859-65 similarly underwent an early crisis due to the controversial budget of 1860. Gladstone, the Chancellor, found that he had a surplus of £5,000,000 early in 1860; instead of using it to abolish income tax, which then stood at 9d in the £, he proposed to raise income tax to 10d in the £, and with the increased revenue to abolish the paper duties. These duties contributed to the high cost of books and newspapers and were much resented by Radicals and working men as an unnecessary 'tax on knowledge'. The Cabinet was divided over Gladstone's proposal, but a majority of members favoured it. Palmerston did not; he wanted to keep the paper duties, income tax and the tea duty, and to allot the revenue to the needs of national defence.

Although the Bill to abolish paper duties passed narrowly through the Commons, the House of Lords threw it out by 193 votes to 104. The Lords, who had accepted the Bill raising the rate of income tax, had not rejected a finance bill for two centuries, and a constitutional crisis threatened. Palmerston,

147

however, was known to oppose Gladstone's Bill. He therefore merely proposed to refer the Lords' action to the Committe of Privileges, thus avoiding the awkward situation of sending the Bill back to the Upper House a second time. He incurred a good deal of criticism for his attitude, going some way towards justifying Disraeli's description of him as 'the Tory chief of a Radical Cabinet'. The issue did not, however, die with the budget of 1860, for Gladstone announced in 1861 that he proposed to reduce the rate of income tax from 10d to 9d in the £ *and* abolish the paper duties; moreover, both proposals would be introduced in the same Finance Bill, and the Lords would thus have to reject the whole Bill (and risk a furious controversy) or let it through intact. Palmerston was extremely annoyed with Gladstone, but the Bill went through and an important precedent had been established.

Palmerston's approach to other matters of domestic concern was fundamentally conservative, though here and there a reforming gleam shone through. This is not to say, however, that overall he was a predictable establishment figure. In the matter of high ecclesiastical appointments, for example, he was decidedly Low Church, but this was chiefly because he relied upon the advice of his evangelical son-in-law Lord Shaftesbury in these matters. Shaftesbury had earlier expressed his misgivings over the prospect of Palmerston's episcopal appointments, complaining, 'He does not know, in theology, Moses from Sydney Smith. The Vicar of Romsey, where he goes to church, is the only clergyman he ever spoke to.' These fears proved misplaced in practice, and the Church of England acquired during Palmerston's premiership its quota of 'Shaftesbury Bishops'.

In the matter of creating peers, Palmerston was both reactionary and progressive – or rather took the same pragmatic view of issues that had previously marked his handling of foreign affairs. He saw the House of Lords as a constitutional bulwark against the dangerous inroads of democracy. Thus he tended to create peers from the ranks of those who, in his opinion, were sufficiently wealthy to sustain their new status, though he favoured loyal Liberals as well. But he did not agree that, say, great academic or artistic achievement merited a peerage; on the other hand, he advocated the conferment of life peerages on new law lords, but the House of Lords blocked this proposal.

He was ready to accept the decimalisation of the currency, and it had been planned that the two-shilling piece, which had been introduced in 1849, was to be one-tenth of a pound sterling. But the decimalisation scheme collapsed because of the expense involved. Although Palmerston looked favourably on this reform he vehemently opposed the adoption of the French system of weights and measures, asking, 'Can you expect that the People of the United Kingdom will cast aside all the names ... which they learnt from their infancy and all of a sudden adopt an unmeaning jargon of barbarous words representing Ideas and Things new to their minds. It seems to me to be a Dream of pedantic Theorists. ... I see no use however in attempting to Frenchify the English Nation, and you may be quite sure that the English Nation will not consent to be Frenchified.'

Palmerston remained deeply interested in matters of national defence which were given added significance during the anti-French alarm of 1859-60. In 1861 he was installed as Warden of the Cinque Ports, and made a speech in which he said that there were only two ways in which a nation could be secure, either by being perfectly insignificant, or by being in a state of perfect defence, 'England will never, I think, enjoy the former'; but he hoped that she would long enjoy the latter. Palmerston's dedication to this cause was only ended by death, and on his eightieth birthday he spent the whole day inspecting the fortifications on the south coast, suffering no greater discomfort than the moist sea breezes washing some of the dye out of his whiskers.

On a wide variety of other domestic issues his views were no more progressive than those of the average Englishman of his times. He favoured flogging for violent crimes, and a statute passed in 1863 made flogging an additional punishment for robbery with violence. He robustly defended capital punishment against those whom he termed the 'benevolence-mongers', and also believed that public executions deterred potential murderers. He opposed competitive examinations to the executive grades of the Civil Service, death duties on land, and the relief paid out by the voluntary bodies that sprang up during the Lancashire cotton famine (caused by the American Civil War) to help workers who had been by-passed by the Poor Law Guardians. He also blocked Gladstone's demands that the urban working classes should be enfranchised, thus providing yet another cause of the conflict between the two men which resulted, so Palmerston said, in so many letters of resignation from Gladstone that he feared they would set fire to the chimney at Broadlands.

The foreign policy of Palmerston's last administration saw him as dedicated as ever to British interests. He was perturbed at French interests in the Lebanon and Syria and tried, on the whole unsuccessfully, to counter them. He also attempted to hold up the building of the Suez Canal, and in 1863 the British ambassador at Constantinople managed to persuade the Turkish Sultan to order the Khedive of Egypt to stop using forced labour in the construction of the canal; but Napoleon III backed up de Lesseps and the Suez Canal Company, and the work went ahead.

Clearly Napoleon III was no Louis Philippe, and Palmerston found it much more difficult to assert himself against the Emperor as opposed to the Citizen King. Naturally there were also opportunities for Anglo-French cooperation. In 1860 a combined British and French expeditionary force marched on Peking to enforce Chinese compliance with all the terms of the 1842 Treaty of Nanking. Palmerston was glad of the chance to 'bring John Chinaman to his bearings', and even approved wholeheartedly of the burning of the Emperor's beautiful and ancient summer palace by the allied troops, remarking that 'it was absolutely necessary to stamp by some permanent record our indignation at the treachery and brutality of these Tartars, for Chinese they are not'. A year later a joint British, French and Spanish force landed in Mexico to compel the government to settle outstanding debts owed to citizens of those three countries. When Palmerston discovered that Napoleon III, in the aftermath of the successful invasion, was planning to place the Austrian Archduke Maximilian on the Mexican throne as a French puppet Emperor, he reacted favourably, believing that stability was needed in Mexico, and that, thus occupied, Napoleon III would be less of a nuisance in Europe. Two years after Palmerston's death, however, Maximilian was deserted by France, and captured and shot by forces of the Mexican Liberal leader Benito Juarez.

Though Palmerston had acquiesced in French plans in Mexico, he was resolute enough elsewhere. In 1863 the presence of British men o'-war off the coast of Brazil in an attempt to stop slave-running resulted in a dockside scuffle involving a drunken British officer. This was followed by the seizure of three Brazilian ships. Palmerston held out against paying compensation to the Brazilian authorities until an unfavourable Belgian mediation obliged him to give way. In the same year, Britain claimed heavy compensation from the government of Japan for incidents leading to the deaths of three Britons; although the Japanese apologised and agreed to pay the compensation, they were unable to produce the murderers, and early in 1864 the Royal Navy bombarded Kagoshima, killing over 1,400 Japanese civilians. Despite protests in Parlia-

151

ment, Palmerston backed the British admiral's action to the hilt.

Britain's relations with the United States, however, required more sensitive handling. The outbreak of the Civil War in 1861 between the seceding slave-owning Southern Confederacy and the Federal government posed awkward problems for Britain. Not least of these was the economic threat posed to the British cotton industry by a successful Northern blockade of Southern ports, from which in peacetime came the raw cotton for the looms of Lancashire factories. Palmerston was sympathetic to the Confederate cause, though less so than his colleagues Russell and Glastone. It was odd, at first sight, that the celebrated anti-slave-trader should favour a slave-owning rebel Confederacy, but, as always, Palmerston was thinking of British interests. He relished the North's early defeat at Bull Run (or as he called it 'Yankee's Run'), and believed that:

> It is in the highest Degree likely that the North will not be able to subdue the South, and it is no doubt certain that if the Southern Union is established as an independent state, it would afford a valuable and extensive market for British manufactures. But the operations of the war have as yet been too indecisive to warrent an acknowledgement of the Southern Union.

Palmerston refused to recognise the sovereignty of the Confederacy, but he went far in other ways in support of the Southern States. He and Russell, the Foreign Secretary, decided to recognise the South as a belligerent and were prepared to receive their envoys –though they were not, of course, able to treat them as official ambassadorial representatives. An early clash between Palmerston's government and that of the newly-elected Abraham Lincoln resulted from the dispatch of two Southern envoys, Mason and Slidell, to Britain and France respectively. The Confederacy wished for recognition from these two powerful European powers, and, if possible, active military support. But Mason and Slidell, trying to squeeze through the Northern blockade aboard a British passenger ship the *Trent*, were captured off the coast of Cuba by the Federal ship *San Jacinto*. Protests poured into Washington from the South and London; Palmerston was prepared to whip up bitter feeling against the North, and an extra three thousand troops were ordered to Canada. But although war was in the offing, tempers cooled and prudence prevailed on both sides of the Atlantic. Lincoln's provocative Secretary of State, Seward, in the last resort wished to avoid war with Britain, and Mason and Slidell were released to continue their journey. Palmerston was overjoyed at this Federal retreat and wrote to the Queen congratulating her on the humiliation of Bright's 'favourite North American Republic'.

Despite Palmerston's prejudices against the Federal government, and the fact that he was soon calling at the newly-established Confederate offices in Suffolk Street, Pall Mall, he had no wish to provoke war with the North, though it is evident that on several occasions he seemed prepared to be drawn into the conflict. A further cause of friction arose in 1862 when a Confederate warship, later named the *Alabama*, was built secretly at Birkenhead and managed to sail from the shipyards despite protests from the Federal authorities and a belated attempt by the British government to prevent her departure. The *Alabama* proceeded to wreak havoc among Northern merchant shipping until hunted down in the summer of 1864. The United States government protested, with some justice, that the British authorities had connived at the *Alabama's* construction and allowed her to slip out into the North Atlantic. Palmerston was unsympathetic to these representations, but seven years after his death Britain paid the United States $15,500,000 in compensation.

Lincoln's proclamation of 1 January 1863 freeing slaves in the rebel states not only swung much of British opinion to the Northern side, but, coming in the aftermath of General Lee's narrow defeat at Antietam, encouraged Palmerston to resist recognising the Confederacy. When the South's most threatening offensive was turned back at Gettysburg in July 1863, and simultaneously General Grant captured Vicksburg in the West for the Federal government, the chance of the Confederacy's managing to establish itself as a sovereign state was dealt a deadly blow. The war still had nearly two bloody years to run, however, during which time Palmerston hoped for Confederate success but steadfastly refused to grant diplomatic recognition to Jefferson Davis's government. When, in the spring of 1865, the Confederacy was being torn to shreds, and triumphant Northern forces led by Generals Grant and Sherman were closing in on the tattered, grey-uniformed remnants of the once proud Southern armies, the Confederate envoy in London, Mason, desperately asked Palmerston if he would recognise his government if it abolished slavery. Interestingly, and quite consistently, Palmerston dismissed this last-ditch proposition by telling Mason that the system of slavery in the South had never been a factor in preventing British recognition.

Abraham Lincoln, President of the victorious North, was assassinated a few days after the collapse of the Confederacy. During Lincoln's momentous tenure of the Presidency, however, Palmerston had first to deal with a European statesman who had just embarked on a career as Minister President of Prussia that was destined to change the course of European history – Count Otto von Bismarck. Palmerston and Bismarck clashed over the Prussian statesman's wish to bring the duchies of Schleswig and Holstein under Prussian and Austrian rule respectively, thus gaining the vital port of Kiel for Prussia. Bismarck planned to seize the duchies in cooperation with Austria, and then (probably) go to war with Austria to take Holstein and achieve a dominant position in the German Confederacy. Then it would be possible to create a unified Germany under Prussian leadership.

Palmerston quite misjudged the Schleswig-Holstein situation. He put his government firmly behind Denmark, which possessed suzerainty over the duchies. In July 1863 he told the House of Commons that Russia and France would join in upholding 'the independence, the integrity, and the rights of Denmark'. He moreover grossly underestimated Prussian military strength and argued that 'the first Serious Encounter between [the Prussian army] and the French would be little less disastrous to Prussia than the Battle of Jena'. But in the event, neither Russia or France was prepared to go to war over Schleswig-Holstein, and when, in February 1864, Prussian and Austrian forces invaded the two duchies, Denmark's appeals for help went unanswered. Britain could not commit herself, without powerful European allies, to an armed intervention. Palmerston, when he saw the realities of the situation, in effect deserted the Danish cause; he was supported by the majority of his colleagues in this prudent, if somewhat inelegant, retreat, and an opposition vote of censure was defeated by 313 votes to 295 in the Commons.

Perhaps it was a good thing that Palmerston's career was drawing to its close. England could not afford to be made to look ridiculous. In effect, a great deal of Palmerston's success was based on brilliant bluff. He had behaved as if Britain was more powerful than all other countries and the extraordinary thing is that he was believed. In areas of the world where sea power could be really effective Palmerston's high-handed attitude had some substance behind it. On the European mainland, however, the simple fact was that Britain did not have the means of influencing events. The pace of war was speeding up; railways meant that soldiers could be moved much more quickly. Campaigns previously lasting years would be over in a matter of weeks. In such circumstances Britain's small land forces could not be expanded in time to have any effect on the outcome of events.

The Schleswig-Holstein débâcle did Palmerston little harm in the eyes of the electorate. In the summer of 1865 he fought a general election which resulted in an increased Liberal majority in the House of Commons. Palmerston enjoyed his usual hustings joust with the indomitable Rowcliffe, who in fact voted for Palmerston's Liberal fellow-candidate Heathcote and for the single Conservative candidate. Palmerston noted this, and chided his old adversary, saying 'Then you did not vote for me, friend Rowcliffe; you preferred voting for a Tory'. To which Rowcliffe promptly replied, 'I did not vote for you, my Lord, for if I had, I should have voted for a Tory'. Palmerston came top of the poll all the same.

But though Palmerston's tenure of the premiership was so triumphantly renewed, his life was drawing to its close during the late summer of 1865. The beginning of October saw him lively enough at Brocket, Melbourne's old home, even climbing railings to test his strength. But on 12 October he caught a chill while driving in his carriage. Instead of going straight to bed, he dawdled through the process of undressing and obstinately took a bath. A serious fever resulted, and he was not expected to last the night. The Queen prepared herself to send for Lord John Russell if the worst happened. Palmerston rallied a little on 15 October, and his hearty appetite rallied with him, causing him to remark after a breakfast of mutton chops and port that it was odd he had waited all those years before discovering what an excellent breakfast it was.

During the night of 17 October his doctors realised he could not live many more hours. When asked whether he believed in the truths of Christian dogma he replied briskly, as if dealing with some querulous envoy, 'Oh, certainly. Oh, surely'. But his mind was on other things, and when he died at last at 10.45 am on 18 October 1865 it was the clauses of the Belgian treaty, not the gospel, that were ringing in his ears.

His death came two days before his eighty-first birthday;

156

shares fell on the Stock Exchange, and the *Times* obituary ran to 13,000 words. The Liberals were firmly in power, and the way was now clear both for electoral reform and for the rise to supremacy of Gladstone, whom Palmerston privately thought would ruin the party and end up in the madhouse. Palmerston's death removed a symbolic figure from British political life and from international affairs. His methods, though never as brusque as his enemies claimed, had often been more appropriate to an earlier epoch, and in his last years new nations and new economic forces were inexorably altering the world he had once cuffed about the ears. Others would have to foster Britain's interests with more discretion. Palmerston was a proud man who led a proud nation. When someone once said to him, thinking to be complimentary, 'If I were not a Frenchman I should wish to be an Englishman', he replied, 'If I were not an Englishman I should wish to be an Englishman'. It could serve as his epitaph.

SELECT BIBLIOGRAPHY

Airlie, Mabel, Countess of, *Lady Palmerston and Her Times* (London, 1922)

Ashley, E., *The Life and Correspondence of Henry John Temple, Viscount Palmerston* (London, 1879)

Baily, F. E., *Shaftesbury* (London, 1974)

Battiscombe, G., *The Love Story of Lady Palmerston* (London, 1938)

Bell, H. C. F., *Lord Palmerston* (London, 1936)

Best, G., *Mid-Victorian Britain* (London, 1971)

Blake, Lord Robert, *Disraeli* (London, 1966)

Briggs, A., *Victorian People* (London, 1954)

Cambridge History of British Foreign Policy 1783-1919 (ed. Sir A. W. Ward & G. P. Gooch) Vol. 2 (Cambridge, 1922-3)

Cecil, A., *Queen Victoria and Her Prime Ministers* (London, 1953)

Cecil, Lord David, *Melbourne* (London, 1954)

Cecil, Lady Gwendolen, *Life of Robert Marquis of Salisbury* Vol. 1, 1830-68 (London, 1921)

Coningham, W., *Lord Palmerston and Prince Albert* (London, 1854)

Connell, B., *Portrait of a Whig Peer* (London, 1957)

Connell, B., *Regina v. Palmerston* (London, 1962)

Dalling & Ashley, *Life of Henry John Temple, Viscount Palmerston* Vols. 1-5 (London, 1870-6)

Edwardes, M., *The Red Year* (London, 1973)

Gash, N., *Mr Secretary Peel* (London, 1961)
  Sir Robert Peel (London, 1972)

Guedella, P., *Gladstone and Palmerston: their correspondence 1851-65* (London, 1928)
  Palmerston (London, 1926)

Harrison, J. F. C., *The Early Victorians* (London, 1971)

Hibbert, C., *The Destruction of Lord Raglan* (London, 1961)

Longford, Elizabeth, *Victoria R. I.* (London, 1964)
  Wellington: Pillar of State (London, 1972)

Lorne, Marquis of, *Viscount Palmerston, K. G.* (London 1892)

Macrory, P., *Signal Catastrophe* (London, 1966)

Magnus, P., *Gladstone* (London, 1954)

Malcolm-Smith, E. F., *Palmerston* (London, 1935)

Malmesbury, 3rd Earl of, *Memoirs of an ex-Minister* (London, 1885)

Marshall, D., *Industrial England, 1776-1851* (London, 1973)

Martin, Kinsley, *The Triumph of Lord Palmerston* (London, 1924)

Marx, Karl, *The Story of the Life of Lord Palmerston* (London, 1899)

Minto, Earl of, *The Life and Letters of Sir Gilbert Eliot, First Earl of Minto* (ed. Countess of Minto) (London, 1874)

Moneypenny, W. F. & Buckle, G. E., *The Life of Benjamin Disraeli, Earl of Beaconsfield* (London, 1929 ed.)

Morley, J., *The Life of Richard Cobden* (London, 1881)

Morley, J., *The Life of William Ewart Gladstone* (London, 1903)

Palmer, A., *Metternich: Councillor of Europe* (London, 1972)

Palmerston, Lady, *Letters*, ed. T. Lever (London, 1957)

Pemberton, W. B., *Lord Palmerston* (London, 1854)

Prest, J., *Lord John Russell* (London, 1972)

Read, D., *Cobden and Bright* (London, 1967)

Ridley, J., *Lord Palmerston* (London, 1970)

Rolo, P. J. V., *George Canning* (London, 1965)

Sanders, L. C., *Life of Viscount Palmerston* (London, 1888)

Schoyen, A. R., *The Chartist Challenge* (London, 1958)

Snell, F. J., *Palmerston's Borough* (Tiverton, 1894)

Southgate, D., *The Most English Minister: the Policies and Politics of Palmerston* (London, 1966)

Stanmore, Lord, *The Earl of Aberdeen* (London, 1893)

Taylor, A. J. P., *Bismarck* (London, 1955)

Trollope, Anthony, *Lord Palmerston* (London, 1882)

Urquhart, D., *Material for a True History of Lord Palmerston* (London, 1866)

Urquhart, D., *The Queen and the Premier* (London, 1857)

Vincent, J., *The Formation of the Liberal Party 1857-68* (London, 1966)

Webster, Sir C., *The Foreign Policy of Lord Palmerston 1830-41* (London, 1951)

Wilks, W., *Palmerston in Three Epochs* (London, 1854)

Woodham-Smith, C., *The Great Hunger* (London, 1962)

Woodham-Smith, C., *Queen Victoria* Vol. 1 (London, 1972)

Young, G. M., *Victorian England* (2nd ed. 1953)

INDEX